The Power & Freedom

Of

P.U.R.P.O.S.E.

A guide to Thirty days of yielding & four days of expanding

DILLON ST. E. BURGIN

1

Published by Rising Stars Outreach Center
www.risingstarsoutreachcenter.com; www.risingstarscommunity.org

Rising Stars Outreach Center (RSOC) was established in 2006 to address the problems of residents of the urban centers of the New York area, particularly the youths. Using the performing arts a s its main tool, RSOC will bring attention to the problems faced by economically deprived and underserved youths; it will also assist these youths in keeping hope alive, through engagement in tangible means of bettering their lives.

Published 2013 in corporation with Dillon St.E Burgin
Brooklyn, NY

Unless otherwise indicated, scripture quotations in this publication are from the Holy Bible, New International Version ©1973, 1978, 1984, International Bible Society.

ISBN: 978-0-578-12794-1

Dedication

This book is dedicated to Grandma Sylvina

Sylvina Horne is my grandmother. She raised me like her last of nine children, since I was privileged to be the first grandchild. She has no more than a third grade education, yet her children rose up and called her blessed. Working as a peasant gardener, she aided each of her children in building themselves a dwelling place.

Acknowledgement

Let me take a moment to express my thankfulness for the encouragement and support of a wide array of generals and foot soldiers in God's service. I am deeply indebted to my wife Carlene whom I often depend on as a sounding board for my thoughts and new ideas. Her critical and honest reflections always enhance my own thoughts.

I am also indebted to my ministerial colleagues, from a wide range of denominational persuasions who allow me to exercise leadership among them. By their example and exposition on some key principles of God's word, they've made me spiritually richer.

Finally, I am eternally grateful for the daily prayers and positive energy extended for and to me by God's foot-soldiers. Their prayers for me and their presence at my events, fuel the hope that I cherish for a better world and a better universal church.

CONTENTS

Preface

This book reflects an evolution of thought on the subject of purpose. It began as an essay and has evolved into this edition of a book called "The Power and Freedom of P.U.R.P.O.S.E." Years ago, I read somewhere that "marriage is a person's last best chance to grow up". With regards to purpose, I say, the pursuit of purpose and the working out or fulfillment of purpose is the most liberating experience one can seek.

Some pursuits in life and some experiences can captivate a person, to such an extent that the person cannot break free, even when he/she tries. Such is the pursuit of purpose and the experience of living in one's purpose. The most amazing thing about purpose is that it holds on to you so tightly. And yet, it is that holding on that actually sets you free. For example, I recently had a conversation with an artist who works tirelessly for long hours every day. He began to complain subtly about the work he has to do. There arose a delight in his voice as he spoke of something that gave him meaning. I immediately said to him, "I'm sure this is the very thing that makes you look forward to waking up each day and starting your day right." He gave a hearty chuckle and replied "Yeah, you're right." That is the essence of purpose.

You may be weighed down by the duty of your gift, calling, and daily tasks in life. Yet without that combination of gift, calling, and daily task; you will be miserable beyond measure. One of my ministerial friends used the previous version of this book as a study tool with his congregation. He later made a startling confession to me. He said, that after reading the chapter on refocusing and retooling, he decided to close his struggling congregation and take a break from shepherding a congregation.

The exciting and redemptive side of the story is that two years after taking such drastic action, my friend opened a new ministry and has seen growth and stability beyond what he had predicted.

So here is my gladsome warning to the careful reader; and the diligent person who will follow through on doing the exercises in this book: It will change your life for the better. And you will be glad it did. Permit me to say in advance, "Welcome to the new, exciting and optimistic you!"

Dillon St. E Burgin

Introduction

"The power and Freedom of Purpose" was first written as an essay in 2003. It was later published as a book called *Driven by Purpose* in 2004. By 2010 it had evolved into an abridged version called *Free in the bondage of Purpose*. Now comes this further evolution of the book. This book is a study guide. It is also a self-help, planning guide to a practical and more productive life.

The growth reflected in the antecedent versions of this book, showed how a person can simultaneously experience a sense of freedom, while at the same time having a deep sense of constraint. This is in line with what Paul of the Bible describes as "The love of Christ constrains us".

In this present form of evolution in my thinking; I am sharing my latest revelation form the Lord. That revelation is: we are set free by purpose. We are not merely free operators within this thing, or this reality, or this mode, or this experience called purpose.

In some strange way, purpose finds you as you seek it. When this finding meets with your seeking, you experience a sense of freedom that gives you a vulnerability that can only be described as a fluid openness to what your divine creator included in the blueprint for your life.

There are actions that I have taken over the last ten years, which have radically changed my life. These actions have calculated to bring me to a point of reflection and introspection. I am more resolute and determined to discover a deeper spiritual awareness and the manifestation of the knowledge which comes from such awareness. This quest for a deeper spiritual awareness with its manifestations, has given me a stronger commitment to living out what I have discovered to be my purpose. At the same time, it has forced me to be more cautious in cooperating with God for my blessings. This means, that I must let God bless me rather than letting myself make a blessing. There is more to this than meets the eye.

My style of choice is the use the word PURPOSE as an acronym. I sincerely hope that you who journey with me through the purpose matrix will be greatly helped in understanding purpose and in being motivated to follow the purpose of your own life. I encourage you to desire this awareness of which I speak.

If you can confidently (and honestly) say that you know what your purpose is, I entreat you to still journey with me, so that you can glean the nuggets of wisdom and the practical recommendations that are noted throughout the pages of this book.

You will find the exercises at the end of each chapter of this book invaluable. Take your time and complete them thoroughly. Whenever possible, meet with a group to study this book and to share your personal journey. This book will only be completed and successful if it encourages, challenges and help you to release the eagle that is shut up within you. So stop being afraid of success and fly.

Your prayerful fellow traveler
Dillon St. E. Burgin

PART 1

Elements of P.U.R.P.O.S.E

Chapter 1

P: Planning, Preparation, Production

Day One

Read, Meditate & Make notes!!

The first "P" in purpose represents a vital three-part element.

First, to speak of planning is to speak of **design, desired outcome** and **strategy.** One needs to visualize a desired end. Such visualization will give rise to ideas, agents, and needs. Planning requires significant mental energies and focus. It also demands a high measure of **personal discipline.** Even more so, it also demands **emotional strength** to face the hidden problems of what you are trying to achieve. This level of emotional strength is needed to face the high level of commitment that fellow workers on the project need to show.

The legacy of King David in the Bible helps us to understand this three-fold process. In the book of II Samuel 7 we read of David receiving instructions from God to build a special temple as a lofty symbol of honor to God. David embarks on the project by planning the dimensions of it and giving the plan to his son Solomon (1Chronicles 28:11). The next thing we know is that David sets preparatory machinery in place. He deployed his subjects and skilled craftsmen to source and to stock-pile the necessary material for the temple (1 King 5:13ff). Eventually the temple was constructed (production took place). The construction was not done by David himself, but by his son Solomon some years later (I King 6: 38). I guess we can also note another important message here; the same person or the same group that initiated the three fold process may not always complete it. Legacy is important. We should start the work and we should leave something for our offspring and our successors to carry on the work with. In fact, where possible, we should leave the means for them to complete what we started. What are you leaving for your children? Nevertheless, if one understands that his purpose is to contribute to the goal in view, then in his own way he will complete the three-fold process many times over. That is to say, **the person who is truly free, will look at the smaller duties as the building blocks for the end product or the bigger goal**. Hence, he or she will plan, prepare and produce many small goals and win many small battles. In other words, the person who is driven by a sense of purpose will always be mindful that big achievements are really a combination of many small ones. One example of this is the process of acquiring a house. First we envisage a picture of the house we would like to own or the house we are willing to settle for, according to our financial capabilities or other determinants. We then hire an architect to put the plan in pictorial form or drawing for us. Although planning may be as challenging as we have just described it, it rewards us with confidence and satisfaction in having a road map and some signposts along the way. That map gives added impetus to the worker who moves to the second step.

The second step is preparation. Once the relevant bodies or committees or boards approve the plan, we can then proceed. In the example of building a house, we go on to negotiate with builders and hardware suppliers. Then we get the material and go to work. In other words, we have moved from planning to preparation. At this stage, we can say that we are giving flesh to the plan.

If planning is considered the map and the direction, then preparation can be thought of as the gathering and the ordering, or laying out of the resources that are needed for production. Planning says how one needs to do a thing and what resources one needs to do whatever that thing is. Preparation on the other hand says, 'here are the actual parts, the tools, and the step by step method for putting them together. Hence, preparation is the acting out or the showing of what the plan says.

We see this pattern in King Solomon's approach to building a temple for God. He received the plan for the building. He then conscripted his subjects to supply the material and the labor for the construction; and they got to work (I Kings 5). Here we see an example of the first two steps – planning and preparation. These steps give way for the end product to be accomplished.

The third step is production. This step becomes the result of the planning efforts and the application of those plans (i.e. the preparation process). An example from our everyday life is the experience of making pastry. Once the baker decides on the kind of pastry that is suitable or desired for a particular occasion, then he or she must decide on which recipe should be used and what modification, if any, should be done to the recipe. The elements for the pastry are then gathered up and combined in a systematic way to ensure the best results. Special care must be given to the order or sequence and timing of adding each ingredient. After steps one and two are completed, the baking machine is prepared and the special pastry is produced for the given occasion. It should be noted that sometimes the three parts of this "P" element in purpose, may have to run concurrently for greater effect. For example, in the case of the pastry, the oven may need to be pre-heated while the final stage of the mixture is taking place.

Nevertheless, great care must be taken not to unnecessarily complicate or short-circuit the process. You must not become impatient. Nor must you disregard the natural flow of the process. This will help you to avoid mixing up the steps and it will ensure that you move towards your end goal.

(STOP) Stop (YIELD) Yield

Day 2

Dreams and Hopes

1. Write a list of the dreams and hopes you have for a preferred future. *In this case restrict your answers to the next five to eighteen months.* Be precise in stating what things in your personal life you would like to change.

_____

_____

_____

_____

2. What precise things in your neighborhood or community you would like to see improve?

_____

_____

15

3. In what precise ways can you help to improve them?

_____

_____

_____

_____

4. Make a list of the commodities, persons, and general resources you will need to accomplish your plans.
[Examples could include scholarships, investments, trained educators, land, etc].
Be precise enough to give names, addresses and telephone numbers. Make your list here:

_____

_____

_____

_____

5. Begin to contact the persons and institutions that will supply the commodities and resources you will need. You may be met with some rejection and denial. Do not let them stop you. Call again. Set an appointment. Make a personal visit. Write what you plan to do next:

_____

_____

_____

_____

     I remember the time that I needed to settle a bill with a large company. I called to discuss the matter with them. The agent on the phone gave me an unfavorable answer. I asked to speak with her supervisor. He gave me the same answer she gave earlier. I decided to end the call. I called back about an hour later. I got a different agent on the phone. He was so courteous and helpful. He gave me a more favorable answer than I was seeking. I was so relieved. I learnt another lesson that day, in how not to take the first "no" for an answer.

6. What do you need to *do now*, that can be a workable solution for your problem and your needs? Even if you have limited time and resources, put them to *work now*. You will need to prioritize. The key to prioritizing is to ask the following questions:
a) What needs to be done now to prevent things from going bad or getting worse?

_____
_____
_____
_____

b) What needs to be done now to cause some other important things to fall into place?

_____
_____
_____
_____

It is important that you prioritize your plans. You may be able to work on more than one thing at a time. Be careful however, that you do not over extend or over *expend* yourself. You are only one person. And you can only do so much within a given time. I use to get involved in a number of committees, forums, boards and task- force.

At some point it occurred to me that I was doing too much to be as effective as I should be in some essential things. As a result of this realization, I took the humbler path of doing less in terms of the number of activities. Consequently I began to do fewer activities and attend fewer meetings. That left me more time to plan and to concentrate with laser precision on getting fewer things done better. Thus, I have learnt to be more effective. I now make it my priority to engage myself in activities that I find most meaningful, strategic and impacting.

7. Apply the formulae and the resources you have received – Start making something happen.
a) Who have you contacted? *(you must give a name of a person and the organization that the person represents)*

_____
_____
_____
_____

b) What did you ask the person for?

_____
_____
_____

c) What have you received? Be specific about the goods, service or advice.

_____
_____
_____
_____

d) How much time has passed since you received it?

_____

e) What have you done since receiving it?

_____
_____
_____

f) How can the goods, service or advice you've received be used immediately for the greatest good?

_____
_____
_____
_____

Stop Yield

Day 3

Small scale & large scale plans

Repeat steps 1 to 5 from the previous day, on both a small scale and on a large scale as the situation and the scope of the plan demands (Here are those steps again):

1. Write a list of the dreams and hopes you have for a preferred future. ***In this second instance, extend or restrict your answer to include the next two to fifteen years.*** Be precise in stating what things in your personal life you would like to change.

_____
_____
_____
_____

This is important for many reasons. Recently, my wife and I sat down to discuss the future of our family. We had an eye opener when we actually write down some unavoidable facts that would remain with us for a long time. In fact those facts would become more acute as time goes by.

For example, we would be steering the age of retirement in its face by the time our sons complete college. We would also have had to put some financial and logistic arrangements in place because we would be improving the quality of our lives, while at the same time putting our sons through college over the next twenty years.

We thus realized that fifteen years is not a long time from now. We need to be pushing ourselves hard and we need to work smarter at this point, so that we would not be caught off guard. Let this illustration help you to see the usefulness of writing down the things that I ask you to write down as you journey through this book.

If you only think about the answers to the questions that I ask in this book, you are both cheating yourself, and you are showing cowardice. You are showing that you are not brave enough to face both the present realities and the future probabilities head on. Here again is the exercise, with the adjustments for a longer term:

a) List three of your most desirable long-term goals (what you will work towards achieving over the next 5 to 15 years)

_____

_____

_____

b) List three medium term goals (next eight months to three years)

_____

_____

_____

c) List three short term goals (next two months to seven months)

_____

_____

_____

The purpose of these questions and guidelines is two-fold. Firstly, they help you see the need for smaller goals and projects. Secondly, they help you to begin your longer journey. You must develop long term goals. However, you must pay close attention to the short term goals also. In fact, you cannot really achieve the long term goals without accomplishing the short term ones along the way.

The order in which the exercises above are placed is intended to encourage you to set long term goals, then medium term goals, then short term ones. The reason for this is that long term goals will force you to devise a road map to it. That road map will need both medium term and short term goals. So get on with it. Have fun as you move to the next level. The next level is: understanding how and what you do.

Chapter 2

U: Understanding

Day 4

Read, Meditate & Make notes!!

The moment one speaks of understanding he/she automatically implies knowledge. Knowledge is very important but it is not in itself power. **The application of knowledge is wisdom. Wisdom is therefore power.** What this means is that there are many people who are proficient in academic matters. They are smart in the books and in theoretical knowledge. However, they may be merely informed fools. For this reason, many educated people do things that show poor judgment, contempt for others, and share folly. The icing on the cake is a verse we find in the bible "The fool has said in his heart, there is no God" Psalm 14:1. It also means that a person who does not have a lot of academia to boast about, but who has seriously and honestly processed life's experiences is likely to be a stream of wisdom. The Bible says that "wisdom comes from God who gives to all people liberally." James 3:13-18

Certainly one must contend that the only way to know if someone has wisdom is by the actions that one does. This is like saying in the words from the book of James "faith without action is dead". We can also say "wisdom without action is dead." So again, for emphasis, let us affirm that wisdom is power. In other word, power is really strategically applied knowledge.

History bears record of the many men and women who were functionally illiterate and academically sterile; yet they were able to mobilize the masses and inspire or fuel great movements for the betterment of the social conditions of their time. This could be seen in the historical records of wars, of mothers against violence, of parents against drunk driving, of advocates for housing for the poor and a number of other areas of social justice. Knowledge is very important. Academic exposure is terrific. But it is the successful processing (i.e. understanding) and the appropriate application of the processed information (wisdom) that impacts the world for good.

Sometimes I tell people that my grandmother had a gold mine which I saw and which I worked in. However, I did not know that I was an integral part of a gold mine because we were still poor. Let me explain what I mean. My family of origin was steeped in farming. We cultivated produce from the lands and we reared animals. Moreover, my grandmother produced various seasonings, pepper sauce, ground spices, chocolate for making tea; and other products. My being a young man in the family, I had to provide more than a fare share of the labor for this enterprise. For a number of years my grandmother produced both the raw material and the products which derived from them. She produced these commodities on a subsistent level and sold to a rather diverse group of consumers. They considered her products to be the best ones available. We even had a couple of hotels and small restaurants as customers. Moreover, some people bought our products and resold them for up to two hundred percent profit.

Certainly, I did a lot of the work that produced the raw material and their byproducts (merchandise). I never understood that I was looking at a big business Indeed I was holding on to a seed that could have grown into a million dollar tree. Yet all I saw was a low level business which was rooted in agriculture. Not to mention that agriculture was seen as a low-grade occupation in which the peasants engaged because they were not educated enough to do something more prestigious.

You see, I had graduated from the most prestigious high school in the country, so why should I subject myself to this un-prestigious occupation? I say un-prestigious because that is what I was taught. My teachers, elders, mentors and pastors should have told me that "the greats" of antiquity were farmers, herdsmen, land owners, and shepherds. My teachers, elders, mentors, and pastors should have told me that when I am closest to the land, I am closest to God.

Fortunately I arrived at a different level (or should I say a higher level) of understanding after I left my community and my country of origin in order to move to another of the Caribbean Island to attend seminary. While I was in seminary, I thoroughly engaged my courses in history, church and development, leadership; and liberation theology. In that engagement, I developed a new appreciation and respect for the people who labor to feed the population of a country.

My history lessons taught me that if any country is self-determined and if it has ambitions of becoming developed, it must put a number of essential programs and systems in place. One such program or system is the ability to feed its people. A system has to be in place to produce enough food and enough agricultural byproducts. In order to limit a nation's dependence on imports; and therefore limit the extent to which that nation can be controlled by other nations or outside forces.

While I was living in the Jamaica, I interacted with people who worked in various manufacturing and service businesses. They helped me to see possibilities for greater business development than I was previously exposed to. Since that time, I have lived in three larger countries including one Central American country and the United States of America. I have never stopped dreaming, envisioning, growing in my understanding and my planning for business and development.

Perhaps the following illustration will emphasize the point I am making. A man needed to have a test done at a medical laboratory. He took a sample of feces with him to the lab to have it tested. When the lab's technician was ready to take the feces from the man, he told the man to put the "stool" on the table. The man, who hails from the deeply rural area of the country, was not used to hearing the term "stool" in relation to feces. So he did what seemed obvious to him. He proceeded to place the bar-stool that was beside the table, on top of the table. The laboratory technician, becoming distraught and impatient with the "un-educated" man, proceeded to paraphrase his instruction and thus instructed the man in common language to "put the 'shit' on the table." The man then clearly understood the instruction and complied. So, understanding is very important.

The application of knowledge is powerful. I believe that **the proper understanding of what a person comes to know, will determine the quality of the way he/she**

applies that knowledge. The Bible vividly speaks of persons who 'see' but still do not see. Also they 'hear' but still do not hear. The gospel writer of the book of Luke puts it this way, in the words of Jesus "people see but do not *perceive*, they hear but do not *understand*" (Luke 13:10-17).

For emphasis, Let us note - The quality of one's planning, preparation and production, is directly proportionate to the level of knowledge which one brings to the table in relation to the goal in mind, or the desired end. More importantly however, the quality of the outcome depends on your level of **understanding.** In other words, the outcome is greatly determined by the level of how you process what you know, while you work on the project or the mission.

I contend that the application of knowledge is what brings power. For example, if a man faints and he is dying; and a well qualified physician stands by and does nothing with the medical expertise he has acquired; the man will die. If however, the physician puts his knowledge to work, he may save another man's life.

Along the way, you will need to revisit and revise the plan and the other elements that lead you towards discovering your purpose. Hence, in the following chapter we will look at is the "R" in purpose.

STOP **Stop** YIELD **Yield**

Day 5

What should you understand?

1. List three things you really do not understand. These are things, which if you understand them, will change your life greatly. The following areas are examples of important areas that you may find helpful.

Complete the following examples:

a) How do I impart certain values to your children? List the values you wish to pass on to your children:

_____

_____

_____

_____

b) Issues about God and faith - is there a God? What is he/she/it like? Why do I not have a closer relationship with God?

_____

_____

_____

_____

c) How is the company I work for structured?

_____

_____

_____

d) How can I get through the politics of my city?

_____

_____

_____

e) Why do I behave the way I do when a particular matter is raised with me or in my presence?

_____

_____

_____

2. Expand your list to look into areas such as:
 a) The dynamics that are taking place in your family.

_____

_____

_____

 b) An area of interest or need that you have. Be specific about the situation at home or at work or some other environment.

_____

_____

3. What is your choice for a career?

_____

_____

4. List your career goals. Your career could change. It may not be the job that you have right now. This question requires that you choose a career. Your choosing will determine how you move forward with what immediately follows this point.

_____

_____

_____

5. Find some suitably competent or qualified person(s) who can help you decide what options exist within your career choice. Be sure to listen a lot. Share openly.

The list below shows some of the helpers you may reach out to.
* List them in order of priority.
*Decide exactly what questions you will ask.
* Give specific names, telephone numbers and addresses.
* You may even write down the direction and the means of transportation to get to that person. The list is as follows:
 - A psychotherapist

_____

- An expert in your field of interest

_____

- A good friend

_____

- Business consultant or entrepreneur

_____

6. Write down your thoughts/your questions/your issues so that you can be clear about what you want from your helper. *[Note: Do not make any assumptions on behalf of the person].* For example, do not say "I will not ask him/her this question nor will I ask for this resource because he/she will say no". It is better to ask and to be told no, rather than to assume no.

_____
_____
_____
_____
_____
_____
_____
_____

7. Spend five minutes in meditation. Ask God what is his direction for you in choosing who you should see first. Then ask when you should see that person. Finally, Ask God to clearly reveal to you what he is saying about the whole issue.

Write down God's answer below:

_____
_____
_____
_____
_____

STOP **Stop** YIELD **Yield**

Day 6

Connection between issues & plans

1. Investigate whether there are any connections between your issues or plans and those of other person(s). For example, how does your dream of making a lot of money connect with your exceptional skill in baking or playing a musical instrument?

_____
_____
_____
_____

The point here is that you should look for ways in which what you like and what you do, can be used in the service of others and in projects with others for profit and for impact. There are times when we miss opportunities, because we do not look for ways to network with other like-minded people. Also, we do not see the value of what we have in context of where we are.

2. Look at people who have excelled in your area of interest. There's a lot that you can learn from them – even the ones who have messed up at some point.

_____

_____

_____

_____

3. Research areas in which your skill can be used as a business. (You can use the internet as a ready and cost effective tool for your research).

_____

_____

_____

_____

4. Write down the issues that you are concerned about.

_____

_____

_____

_____

5. Write down the plans you have.

_____

_____

_____

_____

6. Draw arrows to connect the issues with the plans. Work through the less obvious ones – think outside of your paradigm. For example, if I am passionate about baking, I can find out whether a pastry outlet or a commercial baker is looking for partners or suppliers. Will they be interested in having my product to compliment theirs? In other words, supposed they will be willing to package my products or use my talent under their label.

This example gives a not-so-obvious connection between your gifts and the big opportunity. However, there are some obvious connections which we can make often. For example, if my family has a business. And I enjoy helping with the business.

Why don't I do a course in marketing? This way, I can promote the business and increase profits.

Another example is this – If, I love fashion and designs. It would be profitable for me to go looking for bargains at factory outlets and then sell garments to friends and other relations.

_____

_____

_____

_____

7. Spend ten minutes listening to God as he speaks through your thoughts. Write down any inspiration you receive. Pray to God for guidance as you move on.

_____

_____

_____

_____

Chapter 3
R: Refocusing and Retooling
Day 7
Read, Meditate & Make notes!!

Despite the quality and the depth of understanding one may have, one needs to make the time to give himself/herself to the practice of refocusing and retooling. This takes us to the R of purpose. Refocusing involves some serious and intentional reflection. However, the reflection is not a static or isolated step. It is an ongoing process which emerges and evolves as the refocusing and retooling take place.

What actually needs to happen is that you as an individual must stop at some point in your life and ask the following questions:

A) Where am I now in my life?

_____

_____

_____

_____

B) Am I at the place where I want to be?

_____

_____

_____

C) Why am I not where I want to be and how can I get to where I want to be?

_____

_____

_____

D) What have I done with the opportunities, re-sources and training that I have received; and have I put them to the best use?

_____

_____

_____

E) What mistakes have I made or what decisions have I acted on that I have learnt from?

_____

_____

_____

_____

F) What can I do and what will I do about the answers to all the other questions above?

_____

_____

_____

_____

The questions above comprise step one of the refocusing and retooling phase. This step evokes the answers that give you a picture of the path that you have taken so far, and the direction in which you should go. The change of direction or the adjustment of your pace in continuing in the right direction is what is meant by refocusing.

Many people give of themselves tirelessly. Sometimes they are compensated for their work. Yet even that does not prevent them from becoming so drained and exhausted, that they must pause to retool and to refocus.

When we look at the pattern of Jesus' ministry, we observe that He often retreated to be refreshed. During his time of preparation in the Garden of Gethsemane, Jesus travailed in prayer "till sweat fell from his face like drops of blood" (Luke 22:44). Nevertheless, it was that depth of retreat and refocus that retooled Jesus for; and focused him even more intensely on his mission.

Usually retooling will demand that you make further inquiry into the subject matter in which you are engaged. This could mean that you have to do some reading and research in a particular field of study or an area of relevance to what you are undertaking. On one level, retooling means that you must sharpens your skills and your talents. On another level, you may have to give an opportunity to someone else to let that person bring their own strengths and insights to enhance your strengths and to challenge your perspective. This will help you to gain different insight into what you are doing.

Sometimes people just do not mature in their thinking or grow in their ministries or in their careers, because they do not open themselves to be challenged, especially by what they have not been previously exposed to. So we often hear comments like "We have always done it this way", or "We have never done that before". We cannot stress enough the fact that the global connectedness which we share today necessitates that we give ourselves to being stretched intellectually, socially and spiritually. We must refocus and retool in order to advance.

One of the important lessons I learned from my exposure as an insurance representative years ago, is that the sales representative should not try to end every interview by securing the sale of a particular insurance plan. The sales representative may often need to return to the proverbial drawing board to examine more carefully the information he has about the client, so that he could devise a policy that is best for the client. That is to say, sales representatives were trained to consider more carefully what the client's insurance needs were; and how his/her ability to pay the premiums matched those needs. As a result of that additional examination, the client usually ended up with the plan that best met his/her needs. So even when the sales representative did not get the level or volume of sales he had hoped for; he still got the satisfaction of having closed a deal while at the same time serving his client with integrity.

Refocusing and Retooling together are an absolute necessity for the life that wants to remain free. This twin element will help you to avoid personal burnout, social impotence and the stalling of your education.

When I wrote the previous version of this book, the word "refocus" and "retool" came to mind because I found myself at a cross-road with my denomination. On one hand I had some convictions which I was not prepared to give up. On the other hand I realized that I was in a state of transition and I also needed some time to find healing and to let the spiritual development run its course. In that transition, my emotional and intellectual capacity increased.

For a while, I stepped out of pastoral ministry and I took a secular job. During that period, I tried to discern where the Lord was leading me. I had some times of misery and near despair. But I knew that I had not completed whatever was waiting to be birthed from my womb of possibility and from my years of experience, sowing and pain. I was determined to line up my life with the destiny that I knew was awaiting me. Thankfully things worked out fine. In time they always do.

In fact I still say today, that I think that the transition and the travailing period in my life was the period that the Lord had to use to separate me from some things, some peoples and some circumstances. That separation was necessary, so that he could have planted my feet in higher places. I will encourage any person in pastoral or care-giving ministry to step away from that engagement for a while and to do something that is not directly related to it. You will discover that you are better able to stay in touch with a bigger reality. You will also discover that you are able to sharpen your tools and acquire new ones.

We should aim for a reflective life. A reflective life becomes a life that refocuses and retools itself many times over. Besides this, a person with the noblest intention and potential may be the agent of a grave misfortune if he becomes too inflexible and too "tunnel-focus" or too stubborn to see a better vision. In order to avoid many pitfalls in life, we must become malleable clay in the hands of a gracious and all-wise God. Small wonder that the Bible says you must know yourself because God knows you *(my paraphrased)* -psalm 31:7.

STOP Stop YIELD Yield
Day 8

Silence with strategic forecasting

1. Take ten minutes to be by yourself in silence (turn off the Television, radio, iPod, computer, and all distractions).

Look at the areas of your life, in which you have become "rusty". That is to say, you know that you have slowed down; you have become disinterested, and less efficient than you were not too long ago.

You know that you have exhausted your creativity. Some areas to look at may include: writing, art, culinary skills, public speaking, job and marriage.

_____
_____
_____

2. Make a list of the ways in which you can improve and increase the areas you identified in number one (1) above. For example, take time out, go on a vacation, attend a spiritual retreat, and read a book that is relevant to your field of study.

_____
_____
_____
_____

3. Decide on the most appropriate course of action you need to take. Make the telephone call or the visit to the helping or sharpening agent. These may include: a specific retreat center, a medical Doctor, a fishing trip, attending a series of concerts or games, investment agent.

This is an investigative stage. Look through your contacts, the yellow pages, or your social media accounts.

_____
_____
_____
_____
_____

⬡STOP **Stop** ▽YIELD **Yield**

Day 9

Focus on your Devotion

4. Start your day with devotion. Do some breathing and or other exercises.

Visit the helping agent or take the steps you need to retool yourself and to refocus your mind, spirit and physical abilities. You might need to find a certain book to read on a specific subject; you may attend a seminar; or you may change your environment for a while.

_____

_____

_____

a. Extend this 9th day by giving attention to devotion, church, exercise, getting on a team (sports, social organization etc.).

_____

_____

_____

b. Thank the Lord for your business. Ask him to show you what you can do today to begin a speedy retooling. Ask God for the strength of will to make the first move.

_____

_____

_____

Chapter 4

P: Pride

Day 10

Read, Meditate & Make notes!!

While the Bible states that "pride goes before destruction and a haughty spirit before a fall" (Proverbs 16:18), the life that is set free by purpose, understands that it must embrace a healthy measure of pride. The often-quoted watch word "take pride in what you do" is what we are speaking about here. That is to say, we recognize that one needs to develop a sense of happiness, confidence and vision.

In the Bible, the prophet Jeremiah once made a bold declaration about himself. It is a declaration which should be claimed by every living person. He said that the word of the Lord came to him, saying that God knew him even before he was formed in his mother's womb (Jeremiah 1: 4-8). In other words, Jeremiah was confident and sure of himself.

He was greatly impacted by the revelation that a "big" and supreme creator took the time to pay attention to him even before he was formed in his mother's womb. Jeremiah grew up and went on to rock a nation through prophecy. He challenged the high and mighty as well as the humble and abased. Perhaps Jeremiah had long pondered the words of the psalmist "I am fearfully and wonderfully made" (Psalm 139:14). This is an expression of healthy pride.

I feel this kind of pride vicariously, when I look at a well sculpted man or a well proportioned woman with their toned physique. And to tap it off, I see such a person display reverence for God and a love for other human beings. Jeremiah's words are the kind of words you would say, having an awakening about yourself in relation to God. This kind of healthy pride can be alternatively called confidence, or it can be referred to as 'pleasure in what you are and in what you are able to do.

The opposite of this kind of pride is the kind that can be called arrogance, indiscretion, and stubbornness as is implied in Proverbs 16:18 "pride goes before destruction and a haughty spirit before a fall."

The pride that is being celebrated in this book cannot be a self-seeking, self-gratifying determination to merely stand out from the crowd. Neither can it be the manifestation of belittling arrogance. The pride of which we speak must be a deep sense of well-being, wholeness, joy and satisfaction within one's self. This kind of pride is in essence the thought, the intention and the action of adding wellness, hope and betterment to the lives of others. In other words, good and healthy pride makes your life beautiful and adds to the life of others. We are free enough to really believe that ultimate purpose is God and God's glory. We are also free to accept Pride as the force that drives us to fulfill or to live out God's engineering for us. God has a designer's blueprint for the human's existence. Pride energizes us to live out the details of it. Pride is justified self-respect. It is delight and elation. It is one of the key factors that motivate people towards their calling in life.

⬡ Stop ▽ Yield

Day 11

Inventory of the physical & the invisible

1. List five physical things about yourself that you should feel good about.

Some examples may include words like height, handsomeness, strength, health and your smile.

_____

_____

_____

_____

2. List five invisible things about yourself that you should feel good about.

Your list may include words like: confidence, devotional life, passion, compassion, ambition and your ability to not hold grudges.

_____

_____

_____

_____

3. Try some activities or task that will help you to overcome your fear and vulnerability. For example, sharing an idea with someone whom you know will be brutally honest with you. Write down the results of the activities and task you did:

_____

_____

_____

_____

4. Introduce yourself to a total stranger. In the conversation, you share with them something good about yourself. Do not boast. Do not degrade yourself either.

_____

_____

5. List **ten things** that you have done well or that you have done as good as they could be done.
Your list may include activities such as:

- Preparing a legacy for your family,

_____

- Outreach,

_____

- Academic pursuits,

_____

- Writing, singing,

_____

- Carefulness in spending your time and your money,

_____

- Reaching out to people in need, being a loyal friend,

_____

- Asking for what you want, etc.

Your list may not include some of the things listed above. They are only examples. If however, you choose to use this list as a starter, then you must write down some specific things that fit into those categories.

_____

_____

_____

_____

STOP **Stop** YIELD **Yield**

Day 12

Visits with your mirror

1. Find the following three portions of scripture and recite them to yourself while looking in the mirror:

a) Jeremiah 1: 4-8 – Before I was formed in my mother's womb and before I was consecrated [God] knew me (paraphrased).

_____

_____

b) Psalm 139: 14 – I praise [God] for I am fearfully and wonderfully made (paraphrased).

_____

_____

c) Matthew 10: 31 – I am more valuable than many sparrows or any expensive commodity *(emphasis mine)*.

_____

_____

2. Walk out today:

• With your head erect;

• With your steps sure;

• Carrying a gentle and radiant smile;

• Looking directly in the eyes, anyone who you encounter today;

• Telling yourself that you are special – That there is no other person in the world like you (because that is the truth).

• Having a positive attitude about you and remind yourself that you are not responsible for other persons' attitudes.

* Note 1: Practice step 2 intensely everyday for two weeks. By the end of that period you should begin to feel it be-coming natural for you. It will change your life!!

* Note 2: If you are not quite ready to publicly follow the six parts of step two above; practice them in front of your mirror every day for one week. Then go out in public and practice them. This is very important because there are many people who cannot bear looking at themselves in the mirror.

I have had at least two persons say to me "I don't look at myself in the mirror". When pressed, they admitted to not feeling good about themselves and not feeling that there was anything special about them (or should we say they felt too "un-special") to merit looking at themselves in a mirror.

Chapter 5

O: Offense

Day 13

Read, Meditate & Make notes!!

We should note that it is often more advisable that a person uses a good offense to defend himself, rather than trying too hard to make a great defense. This is not only a note worthy principle. It is actually a necessary ingredient in developing some relationships. Offense is turbulent waters. Nevertheless, let's jump in.

We must always bear in mind that offense is a built in factor of pride. This is true in the sense that the confidence, the joy and the wellness which pride fosters, can sometimes become an affront to a wide spectrum of people. These people, range from those of low self-esteem, to those who are insecure, to those who are self-serving.

In the Bible, we find many instances of offense. In Revelation 12:11, we are told that there was an assault on a group of holy or specially chosen people. Hence they had to resist. Thus it is said of that group "They overcame by the blood of the lamb and the word of their testimony." The inference here is that the confronting expression of one's words coupled with persistence, even to the spilling of the life-giving substance (blood), are sometimes the price required for the fulfillment of one's purpose. Sometimes, we have to fight or offend in order to prevail in a good cause.

Sometimes we see instances in which one person forces his will on another person. Sometimes we see an oppressed people talking back to or taking actions against their oppressors. The New Testament in the Bible records some shocking words said by Jesus to his followers. The first time I came across those words presumably from the lips of Jesus I was flabbergasted. He said, "I came not to bring peace to the earth but a sword" (Mathew 10:34).

Jesus' ministry proved to have been the most offensive and revolutionary engagement the world has known. He did not use a physical sword, but his message and methods of offense cut through the hearts and systems of humankind in a way that a sword would cut through butter.

When a life functions in the freedom that is given by purpose, it offends. It does not always readily move to a defensive position. Offense here should not be confused with blatant rudeness. Neither should it be seen as arrogance, insult, a show off, self-aggrandizement or envy.

A life that is offensive must attack evil in whatever form it is experienced. That life must cause difficulty and discomfort to any expression of that which is unwholesome and unhealthy. Some other examples from the life of Jesus include the following:

a) On one occasion, Jesus is reported to have referred to king Herod as a fox (Luke 13:32).

b) On another occasion he is reported to have bluntly called the spiritual and social leaders (Scribes and Pharisees) of his day, "white washed tombs that are full of dead bones" despites their outer beauty (Mathew 23:27)

Who among us today are the Herods, the Scribes, and the Pharisees? What offensive positions do we need to take towards them that we may influence them towards justice, mercy and humility? Remember the pharaohs, the scribes and the Pharisees were the national, civic, political and church leaders. They were the keepers of the gates and the defenders of the status-quo. They were the interrupters and the detractors of what God was doing in the then world.

Being offensive does not mean that we have to be obnoxious, malicious or condescending. What it means is that we often need to be forthright and brutally honest. It also means that at times, we need to use the language that people understand and even shock them into hearing us.

My friend Henry once told me of how he found himself in one such situation. After he graduated from college he lost touch with his long-time friend Earl. At some point Henry heard that Earl had gotten derailed by the loss of his family and his battle with addiction. According to Henry, the Lord placed Earl on his heart so strongly that he knew he could not find peace until he found Earl and let him know that God loved him, that he (Henry) still loved him and there was hope for a new start. Henry found Earl and tried to be as understanding, cordial and non-judgmental as he could.

After the two men had spent hours together it became clear to Henry that Earl was still in denial about his condition to such an extent that he spoke in glowing terms about his life, his opportunities to help people et cetera. Henry said it suddenly occurred to him that he needed to give his friend Earl a bit of a shock treatment. So Henry, being a Christian and a leader in his church and all, told Earl that he was in denial.

Henry said that he used two curse words/expletives on Earl as he told him point blank that he (Earl) could not be happy in the "blank-blank" condition. Henry told him that he needed to get help immediately. Earl's eyes opened up widely when he heard his friend Henry use curse words – something Henry had never done before with Earl. Henry went on to tell me that the conversation between him and Earl changed completely. The shock worked, Earl dropped the pretense and began to share more honestly with his old friend Henry.

My reason for telling this story is not to offend your delicate sensibilities as a reader. Nor am I encouraging you to use expletives even in trying to solve a difficult problem. However, I use it as a sort of extreme example of how far out on the offensive one may sometimes go in order to achieve the greater good and to change the direction in which a loved one is heading. There are times when the only thing that gets people to respond positively is some mildly extreme measure or some unexpected shocker.

Having given the less than flattering example above, let me give a milder one to further illustrate the point about the vital role that offense plays in relation-ships and organizations. A man who worked with families in a counseling facility shared this experience with me. A little child whose family he was counseling seemed out of control. The child, a little boy, was saying unkind things to some of the adults in the group. His father kept on telling him "be nice, Tim." The child continued to be rude and distracting until the man who told me the story said to the child, "Tim, that's not 'cool'!" Tim hung his head in shame and stopped his misbehaving.

The observation here is that Tim needed to hear the same message from another authority figure but in a way that was more potent; and in a language with which he was familiar as a young person. At that time, "That's not cool" was a popular expression that young people used to shame each other.

Sometimes you just have to take the path of the offensive and not feel bad about it. Your goal here is not to be malicious and uncaring. You must examine your approach even before you act. By doing this, you do not merely react in order to defend your self-esteem. Neither should you merely try to hide a lack of confidence or to mask a compulsive desire to please someone else.

You should be sensitive and understanding. You should season your words with kindness and grace because sometimes you may have to eat them. At any rate, do not be naïve. Sometimes, you would have to wear iron gloves instead of mittens in order to secure the greater good.

Stop ▽ Yield

Day 14

Apologies and Resolutions

1. Think of five major situations in which you have been apologetic, although you were doing the right thing.

_____
_____
_____
_____
_____
_____
_____

2. Make some resolutions about ways in which you can act more appropriately – even if doing so makes you feel uncomfortable.

_____

_____

_____

_____

3. Ask the Lord to give you a tender heart and a tough mind, so that you can act with understanding even when you have to be firm and hard with someone.

_____

_____

_____

_____

_____

STOP **Stop** YIELD **Yield**

Day 15

Pleasure or pain in offending

1. When last were you offensive to someone in the following circumstances:

a). Have you acted out of pride rather than preserving the others dignity?

_____

_____

_____

_____

b). Have you taken pleasure in hurting the other person in retaliation for what they did or said about you?

_____

_____

c). Have you been showing off your skills in someone's presence rather than being helpful or cooperative?

_____

_____

_____

2. Ask the Lord to forgive you for offending someone, out of the wrong motive. Pray for the healing of the person. Call them up and apologize for offending them.

Write out your prayer. This will help you to actually reflect on the situation and get it out of your system. Write down your thoughts:

_____

_____

_____

_____

_____

Chapter 6

S: Selling

Day 16

Read, Meditate & Make notes!!

We hear people advise others by saying things like "you have to sell yourself". In other words, make yourself believable and convincing if you want people to give you some serious consideration, if you want them to give you a break. The Bible says a person's gift makes room for him. The other side of this coin, however, is that we live in a fiercely competitive world that requires us to promote and advertise what we have.

Without promotion and advertisement we may never go as far as our capabilities can carry us. It is an established facts that people who "make it big" in sports, show business, fashion and even in ministry, are the ones who had the right combination of talent, attitude and great publicity.

The idea of selling really has everything to do with promoting, highlighting and going public. In the context of pursuing, finding and working out one's purpose; selling means that we must advertise and publicize. Our talents, our skills, our tangible resources and our vision must be used publicly to bless other people. By exporting and promoting our "products", the person who imports or buys into them causes them to increase. Thus we experience a greater sense of freedom.

I believe that there is a blueprint. I also believe that most of us do not fulfill that blueprint. The reason for this is one of three things; our heredity, our environment and our choices. These can keep us from discovering and from working our purpose out. Sometimes our selling encounters less than ideal situation. When this happens, we may find that we are unable to promote our own interest or to excel.

Other times, we have to operate in some of the most unpleasant and challenging situations. There are many situations and documented cases in which "sellers" had to oppose injustice. In such situations a skillful negotiator or mediator is brought into the situation. As if by magic, the negotiator/mediator finds a way to process and package the demands of the parties involved. The negotiator is able to sell a good compromise to both parties; and they find a way to move on.

In the given situation, the negotiator has to be able to sell himself as a capable and fair third party. He then has to be able to sell the one party's demands to the other. Of course there are times when situations of conflict are not amicably resolved. This often results from the attitude of some gate-keepers who become adamant and unyielding rather than acting in a humane and decent manner.
Even in those situations you need to be able to sell your vision of the higher ground so that everyone can be motivated to seek a win-win option for all involved.

History illustrates this selling principle for us many times over. Sometimes we see glaring defeat, other times we see admirable statesmanship and common sense on display. This is seen whether in the history of the civil rights movement in the United States of America or in the apartheid dynamics of South Africa, or in contemporary struggles between multi-level corporations and trade unions. The argument here is, the affected or concerned persons in a given situation intentionally sell the vision of a better way and simultaneously they sell (i.e. they **promote and highlight**) the shortcomings of the way things are. This means that we must act in order to change things from what they are into what they ought to be.

The rule of thumb is, that we should always maintain a creative balance between the already and the not-yet, by constantly selling a picture of how beautiful the not-yet can be. Even when the wrong and sometimes "quick fix" thing is done initially, persistently selling a vision of a better way, eventually results in the materializing of that better way.

When all is said and done, we ought to note that the life that is set free by purpose is often misunderstood because it lines up with high aspirations, deep intensity and noble intentions. These qualities can cause people to misinterpret, distrust and even assault you. We find many examples of this in the Bible. For example, after Jesus began his public ministry at age thirty, people began to raise questions about Him:

• Some people asked; "Is not this the carpenter's son?" (Matthew 13:55)
In this case they were challenging him on the basis of his humble beginning.

• Others asked whether his display and work in the temple betrayed "some new doctrine." (Mark 1:27) – In this case, the people were challenging his motive, his orientation and his unconventional approach to God's business.

• Others accused Jesus of being a wine bibber (Like 7:34) and the associate of the prince of demons (Matthew 9:34) because he ministered to the drunks and the outcast and he freed the people who were possessed by demons.

Going public or selling is one of the greatest challenges of the life that is being freed and empowered by purpose. Nevertheless, this is the most tried and true method to help us to create an impact on other peoples. It ignites the search and pursuit of purpose in them. Second to the life of Jesus, no greater example of this kind of marketing is found than what the Bible records about the early disciples. For example, the renowned Christian leader Paul was a man who initially persecuted Christians. He was passionate, brutal and relentless in destroying them in every which way.

Paul however, was somewhat convicted by the aggressive "marketing" of the Christian message which they promoted both by their lives and by their words. Paul was therefore prepared (at least inwardly) to respond to the un-nerving and spectacular movement of God in his life. The Bible says that he was struck down by a light from heaven. And in that moment, he accepted the fullness of the Christian message and the Christ whom the Christians preached.

Paul's response to the voice he heard at the time of that arresting experience. He asks, "Who are you Lord?" Acts 9: 4. In his later life, having had that experience Paul declared, "for me to live is Christ and to die is gain" Philippians 1: 21. He had found his purpose having been made to search himself. He found the highest meaning in finding his place in the heart of God. The new found discovery was so profound and revolutionary that he abandoned his brutal mission and took on a Christ-like one. On this new mission, he understood himself to have received a message from God for the good of the whole world. Paul was sold out to a new master. He then became the best seller of the new religion and relationship he has discovered.

STOP **Stop** YIELD **Yield**

Day 17

Your resources & possibilities

1. Look at your resources, your ideas and the possibilities around you. Make a list:

_____

_____

_____

_____

_____

2. Ask yourself whether you are ready to expose those resources, ideas and possibilities to outside or public scrutiny and input. Timing is crucial. So consider this carefully. Delay is as bad as acting too soon. Write your thoughts and the resource you are willing to expose:

_____

_____

_____

_____

_____

3. List the resources, the ideas and the possibilities. For example a social project, starting or developing a business, founding an institute, and investing in a project. In terms of skills you may look at your ability to write, talk, administrate, organize, etc.

_____
_____
_____
_____
_____

4. Who are the key players in the situation that you wish to address? The list may include your boss, a particular committee or Board (local, municipal, state etc.), financier. List the positions and the actual names:

_____
_____
_____
_____
_____

4.1. List the name again. This time, you must also list their strengths and weaknesses?

_____
_____
_____
_____
_____

* Weaknesses you need to consider could be things like: short sightedness, long delays and a lot of red tapes.
Make a list:

_____
_____
_____

* Strengths may include: solidarity of the organization or the individuals you have to work with, and the level of commitment that your key people have to your project.

_____
_____
_____
_____

4.2. What is the best time to invite them on board?
List the name again and place the timing next to the name.

_____
_____
_____
_____
_____

STOP **Stop** YIELD **Yield**

Day 18

Making calculated moves

1. Examine your opportunities and make a calculated move.
Note – your move is the action part of what you need to do.
Do not seek to take advantage of every opportunity. Look for the best opportunities rather than the good ones.
First, list the opportunities:

_____
_____
_____

Second, plan the moves precisely:

_____
_____
_____
_____

2. Now take your inventory up one notch. You must know yourself. Know whether you are better as a team player or as a "lone-ranger", so to speak. Say it out aloud. Here yourself saying it.
- How does that feel?

_____
_____

- Does it feel accurate and good?

_____
_____

- Or do you need to think about it and make a change?

_____
_____

Find a way to work the two approaches together without letting one displace the other to the detriment of your goal you are trying to achieve. This can be a challenge.

I know what this is like. I myself am always striving to maintain a creative balance and tension between working alone and working with the pace of a team. Sometimes I would give someone a project to do; and that person requires so much of my time and my personal input that I find it easier to just take back the project or task and do it myself.

There are other times when I can see the inefficiency of the person or team that I give a task to do. Yet, I would not get too deeply involved if I do get involved at all. Instead I will give the person or team the opportunity to fail in order that they may get an important point or come to a desired realization.

3a. Pray, asking God to give you the honesty that you need, in order to accept what your true weakness is. Ask God to show you what to do about it. Let him show you the ways of developing the weak areas.

_____

_____

3b. Thank God for your strengths. Work on them today. Focus on them a lot, so that you can live in the zone of your strength rather than being shamed and limited by your weakness.

* Write down your prayers. *Watch what happens as you put those words on paper!*

_____

_____

_____

_____

_____

_____

Chapter 7

E: Exchange

Day 19

Read, Meditate & Make notes!!

Here is a story from my family of origin. My grandmother, Sylvina, is a very generous woman. Nothing she has is too good to give away if someone needs it more than she does. She believes that if she responds to the needs of others, God will supply her own needs. She has proven this to be true more times than I could count. When I was a younger man living at home with my extended family, the children and grandchildren would sometimes get upset with my grandmother for the same thing time after time.

My grandmother who still continues to do some gardening to this day would always give away the best of the produce to certain unexpected visitors who stop by the house to say hello. Sometimes it was the family's pastor or a friend out of the area who stopped by to say hello. When they were ready to leave, Sylvina would give them a package containing the best breadfruit or the healthiest looking ground provision. These would be supplemented by a big bar of chocolate for making tea, a big bottle of all-purpose seasoning, a bottle of pepper sauce; and any other agriculture item or byproducts that was available.

In response to our concerns and displeasure at her giving away her best, Sylvina always had the same profound answer. It took us many years to really understand the significance and profundity of her response.

Her words were "leave me alone. I do not know who will do "good" for my children." In other words my grandmother was saying to us, "I am making an investment. I am laying up treasures for you, but you cannot see it now". In the scriptures, this principle is called "sowing a seed". The problem with many Christians is that we are often in such a state of need, that we eat the seed rather than sow it. Consequently, we do not reap a harvest.

Years later when some of us grew older and moved out to live on our own, and we established our own families, we received so much from the generosity of others that we wondered "why me?" I think of when I served as a pastor in Central America, I was responsible for two churches. I preached at both of them on most Sundays. There was always a particular family who ensured that my wife and I (our family had not yet expanded) were refreshed before we leave for the second service. Moreover, there was always a family that ensured we were nourished after the second service.

Even with all this, it was not until we moved to New York that I really saw the multiplication effect of what Sylvina had invested. People who were virtual strangers gave us of their best to help us settle in. And when my wife and I were having our first child we were blown away by the outpouring of tangible love and goodwill towards us.

Years before I saw these blessings in my own life, I had heard similar reports from the older members of my extended family who were either living overseas or who were seeing the favor of the Lord in their work places. At some point we all had to arrive at the same conclusion. We concluded that we were reaping the harvest from the great seeds grandma Sylvina had sown. As human beings, we are social and inter-dependent. I think you can say, that the person who is truly free has as his/her hallmark, the qualities of mutual acknowledgement and tangible love towards others. To put this another way, a person in pursuit of his/her purpose is deliberate and determined and has a deep social consciousness. This consciousness naturally finds expressions in social involvement for the ordering of a better society. In a real sense, I am not well if you are not well. And you are not well if I am not well.

Some years ago when I was an insurance salesman, I came across this statement - "the greatest act of selfishness is giving." This statement underscores a point of ancient wisdom that what a person gives out returns to that person directly or to that person's descendants indirectly. The wisdom here is that when you do goodness for others you are actually making an investment, or doing something good for yourself. In the life that is set free by purpose, interdependence is regarded as a matrix of interpersonal dynamics. Such a person understands that in the exchange of words, values, energies, space and time people build up each other and truly live. So each of us is a layer upon which others can build themselves. Thus mutual acknowledgement and affirmation become well established and we move together towards the fulfillment of the blueprint for all of humanity as a unit.

The Bible tells of a prophet named Elijah who was sent by God to a widow who, with her son, was on the last of the supplies which they had to make a meal. The prophet, inspired by God, asked the woman to prepare him a meal. The woman did so willingly, though with a measure of despair because there was starvation in the land and she had no hope of finding supplies for another meal.

Despite her predicament, the woman gave of what she had and miraculously the prophet became an agent of ample supply for the woman's family (I Kings : 17).

Many other examples of the returns that one gets as a result of giving or sharing can be found in volumes of recorded stories from different sources. Yet you cannot find a more profound statement about the principle of exchange than this one – "What a person sows that he/she shall also reap" Galatians 6: 7.

The life that is set free by purpose, understands that every person truly needs each other with the resources that each has. Invariably when exchange takes place, the production of tangible and intangible commodities will result.

STOP Stop YIELD Yield

Day 20

Examine your attitude towards giving

1. Spend half an hour making an examination of your attitude towards giving. Do you prefer to receive or to give? *[You should try this exercise with your lights turned off and without any music or other distractions]*.

_____

_____

_____

2. During the course of the day, give away yourself (your money, your time, your skills and talents). And even though you may be busy, give away some of your time.

Plan some likely circumstances in which you will do this. Also, go out with an openness to instances in which it may just happen. Make notes:

_____

_____

3. Make an agreement with yourself today, that you will hold on to things loosely. Tell yourself that you will not worry about the gadgets you lose or the big material things that escaped you.

_____

_____

4. Thank God for what you have. Thank God for all who have given you something that has helped you to reach where you are at this juncture of your life.
Write out your prayers. You will be amazed at what this time of appreciating God will do for you.

_____

_____

_____

_____

STOP **Stop** YIELD **Yield**

Day 21

Giving & permitting yourself to receive

1. Find an institution that you will serve over this week as a volunteer. Find at least two needy children over the next month for which you will do something important. For

example, you may teach them to read or to make some kind of craft. Take time today to look up their information. Call them up and make an appointment.

List the name and contact information of the institution. Also list the contact person.

_____
_____
_____
_____

2. Allow yourself to be hugged today.

    - Accept the compliments others give to you

    -Accept a gift from someone who just wants to show you some appreciation even if you do not need it or even if you can afford it yourself. At the end of the day, make some notes in the space below:

_____
_____
_____

3. Thank God for all whom you have help. Ask God to help you to serve, not out of mere pride and guilt; but out of gratitude for God's gifts and blessings.

[Write out your prayers. You will be amazed at what this time of appreciating God will do for you].

_____
_____
_____
_____
_____
_____

PART 2

The God Dimension of P.U.R.P.O.S.E

Chapter 8

Where Does God fit in?

Day 22

What God?

We have had an exciting and soul searching journey. Now here is your opportunity to do some observations and to apply the principles from your journey thus far. You are encouraged to apply the lessons that you have learnt through the exercises that you did in the preceding chapters.

Purpose relates to God.

First of all, we observed that ultimate purpose is God, the creator of the universe. Every civilization that the earth has known has sought to connect with some kind of superior being. In its bid to make such a connection, each civilization has discovered through intuition, reason and revelation that the Supreme Being is not an object. It is 'being' itself. Hence, we acknowledge that there is the presence of God in everything known and unknown to us. With such mind-boggling concept and discovery, the human being has forever been seeking to maximize its connection to that "being" itself. We have tried to connect with God through the pursuit of various goals and aims.

Write out your answers to each of the questions below. Even if you have done a similar exercise before, still write out the answer. You may arrive at the same answers or some very different ones. The thing you do not want to do is skip the question. That is the one sure way of ignoring the mental and emotional effort that you feel you need to give to these serious questions.

1. Why do we exist? Make this personal. Answer this question – why do I (your name) exist?

_____

_____

_____

_____

2. Why am I here – born into this family, born in the part of the world where my mother gave birth, born at the time that I was born, having the experiences that I have had?

_____

_____

_____

3. Why has life been continually given to me so that I could exist with all that I have known and experienced?

_____

_____

_____

These are the most important questions that you can ask, in the pursuit of your freedom. Your search for meaning will be pursued relentlessly; and it will culminate in your discovery of true freedom.

Jesus is God of Purpose

Since we observed that the pursuit of purpose is directly related to the acknowledgement of a creator, then we have taken it as a given, that there is indeed a creator with which the human being can connect. This way of reasoning may seem illogical or too speculative to some people, were it not for the documented incidents of the prophets, sages, holy men and women; and ultimately of Jesus.

According to the Bible, Jesus is the only human being who has made the bold claims that he made concerning Himself. What do you think about Jesus? If you were to write a paragraph to express your thoughts about Jesus, what are some of the words you will use? Will you say he was a teacher, a good man, an exceptional human, an avatar, a fake, a historical figure whose real story was exaggerated???

Write your paragraph below:

_____

_____

_____

_____

_____

Now that you have written down your thoughts; answer this important question: How much of what you wrote down are your own thoughts; and how much of it is a representation of what you learnt from what you've heard along the way? What does that tell you about the way we formulate our thoughts. Write your answer:

_____

_____

_____

_____

Jesus claimed that He is God (John 1:1- 14 see especially verses 9-14) *"The true light that gives light to everyone was coming into the world. [10] He was in the world, and though the world was made through him, the world did not recognize him. [11] He came to that which was his own, but his own did not receive him. [12] Yet to all who did receive him, to those who believed in his name, he gave the right to become children of God— [13] children born not of natural descent, nor of human decision or a husband's will, but born of God". [14] The Word became flesh and made his dwelling among us. We have seen his glory, the glory of the one and only Son, who came from the Father, full of grace and truth".*

Jesus declared Himself to be truth and life itself (John 14:6). He claims to have the ultimate antidote for the sinfulness and suffering in the world. He epitomize love and miraculous powers in a manner that no other person who has ever walked the earth is known to have done in the same way. What are your thoughts?

_____

_____

_____

_____

🛑 Stop 🔻 Yield

Day 23

Purpose is a Thermometer

Jesus of Nazareth makes a convincing case for His being God the creator and redeemer of the world. We have ample and great reasons to believe this. It stands to reason therefore, that if Jesus is the essence and revelation of God, then Jesus is indeed the God of purpose in two ways:
1) He is the God who has placed within us a "pull" to-wards purpose and

2) He is the God with whom we can find a connection that gives us a sense of direction. The direction we need is towards finding the fulfillment that comes from purpose.

When we embrace this teaching, and when we embrace Jesus in a personal way, we find a unique direction in pursuing purpose. We get into something that calls and drives us. We discover something more than goal: - an end, a result.

This something stands tall in our spirits as a thermometer that is responding to something outside of itself. We eventually get to realize that, that outer attraction, that impacting agent, and that drive is, God – purpose itself. The pursuits of our lives therefore become a measurement of the depths of the connection that we seek with God.

* Reflect on your relationship to God and Jesus. What hinders you from a more personal relationship with God and Jesus? Ask them to draw you closer to them.

_____
_____
_____
_____
_____
_____

(STOP) **Stop** (YIELD) **Yield**

Day 24

Traffic signs of purpose

Purpose has several signs along the road to it. These signs let us know where we need to go. They also explain to us how the world in general works. If we do not participate in these areas we will be at a lost as to what happens around us and to us. If we do observe them and abide by their direction, we will experience substantive fulfillment in life. Notice that the list gives some broad categories. These categories cover all the other smaller or narrower areas of life that we could list.

1) S = **Sociality**

Socially, we dread loneliness more than anything else. We do everything we possibly can to cushion or to defy the effects of loneliness. Even when we "crave our own space" we cannot stand loneliness. We can be alone for a while, but 'aloneness' soon ushers in loneliness. We quickly learn more of our need for others; and we seek company.

2) S = **Spirituality**

Spiritually, we become acutely aware of the void that is within us. We feel the need to settle in our minds and hearts the question of death and the longing to feel wholeness and oneness with God. Many people choose different routes to arrive at that point of peace. Some finally give in to hopelessness or even recklessness after trying many routes, but not arriving at the point of true peace.

3) P = **Politics**

Politically, people seek to influence others for various causes. Those causes may be selfish or altruistic. Some people believe that they will experience fulfillment and inner rest if they are able to manipulate systems and individuals. The goal of such manipulation is to get themselves to the mountain of power, fame and fortune. So the attraction of high places becomes their end in place of the Creator who made the high places.

4) E = **Economics**

Economically, people aspire to the place of might. In this place, in which they can control systems and individuals by withholding or by supplying needed resources in response to the demands. The strength of money is important here. It promises both security and a means of offense in the hands of anyone who acquires much of it. Its lure is tempting, its service is sweet, and its bite is painful. Indeed the power that is locked up in money and other material resources promise its possessor a taste of glory. Money enables you to exercise God-like power as a provider for those who are in need.

In the four ways outlined above, you can see a search for purpose. Again I contend that these four areas must be pursued in some form and to some measure, as a way of discovering ones purpose. However, each must be seen as both and end in themselves; as well as a means to an end. The ultimate end is God. And connecting with God, is the opening of the door to purpose.

*** Decide *what action group you are going to be a part of. Sign up today*. Make a list:

_____

_____

_____

_____

_____

_____

Chapter 9

Mistakes

Day 25

I do make them

People can often mark themselves too harshly because of the mistakes which they have made. And often, these mistakes are made with the best of intentions and with reasonable care. This problem is so common that I choose to address it here. It invites us to mature in our thinking. Such maturing is easier said than done. It is hard because we are more often than not, unforgiving or ungracious towards the faults in both ourselves and others. One needs to understand and courageously work through the scourge and horror of mistakes. In doing so you may likely discover that mistakes are not so bad after all.

It is important to make healthy, calculated, wholesome mistakes. The Bible says that you can do all things through Christ who strengthens you (Philippians 4:13). Unfortunately however, many people deliberately take license to do things that they know are malicious and detrimental. This is the mistake of mistakes. It is nothing more than deliberate folly with unreasonable and false expectation. For emphasis, let us note again that what I call an error is much milder than a mistake. A mistake is more intense, it is characterized by willful blindness and by the determination to do "bad", despite the facts before you. Carefully provide answers to the following questions:

1. What actions have you already taken?

_____

_____

_____

2. How are you moving on after your last big mistake?

_____

_____

_____

3. Think of three errors that you have been making re-peatedly – they will soon become mistakes if you do not stop them.

_____

_____

_____

_____

4. Think of **three mistakes** that you have made in your entire life – that is, three very important things that you did badly or that you were wrong in doing or that you did out of ignorance, innocence or naivety.

Your list may include: lust, greed, your leadership in a group or organization, your role on a team. Make your list below:

_____

_____

5. Now look at how you handled the mistakes you noted above. On a scale of 1 to 7 with seven being the highest score you can get for doing well, how will you mark yourself?

_____
_____
_____

6. Honestly ask yourself whether you did all that you could do to help you move on from the effects of your mistakes. If your answer is no, then examine your present situation and see what more you can and need to do. Seek the help of a trusted friend or helper if necessary.

_____
_____
_____
_____
_____

Preamble to the next three days

Over the next three days you will be asked to examine three common office element or tools. Let the lessons from them lead you to a serendipitous, eye-opening experience. Let this experience change your direction once and for all. Now let us look at the Eraser, the paper-clip, and the post-it-pad. Let these office elements help you to process your mistakes for your own sakes and for the sake of others also.

(STOP) Stop (YIELD) Yield

Day 26

The Eraser – *some mistakes are erasable*

The eraser is a common office supply that sits right there on every desk. It tells us that mistakes are inevitable. So we must prepare for it. It also reminds us that some mistakes are erasable. There are mistakes we make in life which we can correct or which we can nullify in order that we can move on.

Let's take Jane for example. She became a mother at the age of eighteen. She decided that she did not want to carry out motherly responsibilities. So she abandoned her baby. At age forty-five, and now a Christian, Jane is overcome by guilt from her teenage choice. Jane was advised by her counselor, to retrace her steps and find her abandoned child. Jane sought to mend the hurt caused by the abandonment. She found her daughter, and befriended her grown child. Jane asked her daughter for forgiveness and understanding. They became friends and both experienced healing.

In my own experience, my mother left me in the care of her family of origin. Like many young parents in her situation at the time, she immigrated to another country to seek "greener pastures". Fortunately for me my mother kept in touch by phone and by letters. Moreover, my aunts, my uncles and a few family friends cared for me and they ensured that I knew that I was not abandoned by my mother. Years later when my mother thought that I was old enough to understand, she herself had that conversation with me on one of my visits with her.

That conversation was a healing experience for me. It brought some healing to my mother also. Unfortunately however, she has held "her going away" against herself more strongly than I think she should have done. I once asked her to let us start over again as friends, since the years of mother-child nurturing had passed. Over the years we have done a fine job at this.

1. What mistakes have you made that you can erase? Make a list:

_____
_____
_____

2. How can those mistakes be erased? (say what concrete things you will do to erase them:

_____
_____
_____

3. Put a timeline on each of the mistakes. Write down dates and time of day that you will deal with those mistakes. Are others involved? If you need to make an appointment with them, write down the exact time that will schedule yourself to call them. Also write down the slots in your schedule when you will reach out to those persons to erase the mistakes or to begin the process.

_____
_____
_____
_____
_____

STOP **Stop** YIELD **Yield**

Day 27

The Paper Clip – *be flexible with your mistakes.*

The paper clip is also a very common and essential gadget. The wonder of the paper clip is that it is a flexible piece of wire. Its flexibility allows it to be bent into a shape that gives it the ability to hold paper together. The paper clip teaches us that if we are willing to be flexible, there are many things that we will be able to accomplish. The central application we can make from the paper clip is this - you will make mistakes but if you are flexible, they will not crush you. You will find other ways of expressing yourself and starting over.

This kind of flexibility can be seen in the life of the young woman who aborted her baby when she was a teenager. The memory of that action haunted the young woman for a number of years. She lived feeling dirty, unkind and unforgivable. She was finally freed of her anguish and regret after making some important adjustments to her life. She first committed her life to Jesus. After this, she underwent a period of psychotherapy. She then began to volunteer in an orphanage; and she joined a pro-life group in her town. She had reinvented herself and turned her pain into an asset.

1. What mistakes have you made, about which you can change your mind and attitude? In what ways can you make some adjustment and make some compromises?
Make a list:

_____
_____
_____
_____

2. Put a timeline on each of the mistakes. Write down dates and time of day that you will deal with those mistakes. Are

others involved? If you need to make an appointment with them, write down the exact time that will schedule yourself to call them. Also write down the slots in your schedule when you will reach out to those persons to tell them of your compromise and your adjustment.

List the actions to be taken and the timeline below:

_____

_____

_____

_____

_____

_____

_____

(STOP) **Stop** (YIELD) **Yield**

Day 28

The Post-It Pad – _Make use of your permanent mistakes_

The post-it pad is one of the handiest pieces of paper around the office. It comes in a variety of colors. But not many persons know that the glue on the post-it pad is the only one of its kind in the world. It sticks on any surface – whether fabric, wood or metal. And amazingly that glue was the result of a mistake. The central thing to note about the post-it pad is this – you will make mistakes, but if you are willing to re-examine and to probe those mistakes, your mistakes can be the best things that have ever happened to you.

Some mistakes are your biggest blessings. Take for example the man who ate and drank all the wrong things, despite the doctors' orders. That man suddenly found himself lying in the hospital bed helpless and in pain. He later recovered after intense treatment. He subsequently changed his life-style, started exercising, and removed from his diet certain foods that he thought he could not do without.

His dietary mistake almost cost him his life; but that is what it took to make him reach inside of himself and drew out the will power to change his life-style.

Another example is the one involving Susan. She was a young adult woman who lived recklessly. She contracted HIV/Aids. She was full-bodied and voluptuous. The tell-tale signs of the disease took its toll on Susan; and the doctor's report confirmed that she had full blown Aids. She had less than six months to live. Susan went through a period of depression, anger and guilt. During that period she sought the necessary spiritual and social assistance that enabled her to take some positive steps. Among the positive things Susan did were the following: She discussed the matter with her immediate family; she gave legal custody of her eight-year-old daughter to her older sister to whom she also signed over her job benefits; she started spending a lot of time with her two children – eight-year-old Mary and twenty year old Glen.

Susan had just discovered the joy of walking in the park with her children (when she was able to). She also discovered the joy of spending quality time with her family, and the sense of wholeness in becoming attuned to God. She saw that there was wisdom in investing for her children's future by taking out endowment insurance policies for them. Indeed Susan had learnt the hard way that her middle manager's status with all the perks and six-figure income were not the most important things in life. Her big mistake had turned the light on in her family, but she was not going to be around long enough to enjoy much of its glow.

1. What mistakes have you made, about which you can do nothing at this point? This is a mistake that cannot be changed, such as murdering someone, destroying a marriage, blaming your relative for something which you only know was not true after the person was dead and gone; etcetera.

Your assignment at this point is to look at what that experience has done to you. Now how can you use that experience to be a blessing to someone or some cause?

The point here is that you know that you are not the same person. You also know that things are not the same. So what will you do about the change that you cannot now undo or change back? Write down your answer.

_____

_____

_____

_____

2. Put a timeline on each of the mistakes. Write down dates and time of day that you will deal with those mistakes. Are others involved? If you need to make an appointment with them, write down the exact time that will schedule yourself to call them. Also write down the slots in your schedule when you will reach out to those persons to tell them of your compromise and your adjustment.

_____

_____

_____

_____

(STOP) **Stop** (YIELD) **Yield**

Day 29

Find Your Secret Place

Here is a list of some "to dos" that will help you to move some steps further than you have already gone. You may need to become more assertive. You may also need to be more intentional about promoting your gifts and services.

1. Make a move. Take action towards amending your situation. Whether it's correcting the mistakes or making the next move forward. Examples may include setting deadlines or reviving your efforts in getting a project completed.

2. You may encounter some difficulties in retracing your steps and trying to make up for the mistakes that you have made. Here are six useful suggestions of how you deal with them:
• Do not give up at the first sign of trouble.

• Cry if you have to (real men do cry too)

• Become a fool if you have to. This means that you may need to swallow your pride and do something that is necessary even though you may not want to go this route.

• Make sacrifices if you cannot move forward without them. You may need to give up something. You may need to reorganize your time and your involvement in some groups or ministries. This will help you to do what you really need to do and not just what you are comfortable doing.

• Find a quiet place to just relax. That place may be at a swimming pool, a garden, your family den, your bedroom, a retreat center or a host of other places. Spend the time pondering, grieving, reflecting and strategizing so that you can move on again. You may find some soothing and soft music helpful; as well as you may find total silence more helpful.

* *Verbalize* your thoughts or *write* them down. You may choose to discard the paper or notes after you have written down your thoughts. Verbalizing or writing down your thoughts will help you to process those thoughts.

_____
_____
_____
_____
_____

This whole process will put you on your way to erasing your mistakes, that is to say, making amends for them. It will help you to adjust your present life to deal with the mistakes you cannot amend. You will also be helped to use some of your mistakes to create for yourself a better, more efficient and more beautiful person. Know that as you go through this process, your tasks, your services, your occupation and your vocation will benefit.

I took the fourth step a while back. Then about two years ago I took it to another level. I decided that I was not making the best use of my time, and I was not getting out of life all that I really desired. I was busy running to and fro helping people on their boards and committees, making others look good and helping them to achieve their goals. But I myself was not moving ahead; nor was I getting the reciprocal support that I deserved.

Consequently, I informed a number of people that I was being stricter with my time. I concluded that time was my most valued commodity. Hence I had my name removed from some organizations. I then placed my own demands on myself. I began to use my God given time more constructively. I have even noticed that I have developed more impatience with other people who waste God's time by starting functions too late or holding meetings longer than necessary. In the next chapter, we will revisit the steps to purpose.

(STOP) Stop (YIELD) Yield

Day 30

Giving a definitive answer

This is the point at which you are asked to give a definitive answer to the question. What is your purpose? This is a final challenge to give you an opportunity to convince yourself that you are no longer living life by a model that was designed for you by a system, or by society or by some individual without your permission. This is an opportunity to decide once and for all that you will no longer be defined merely by what you do to make a living. You know what your blue print has registered and you are ready to live that out fully.

1. Do you know what your purpose in life is? State it:
Do not be too quick to say yes. The question is open. It does not say anything about your **occupation/job.** Your occupation or your job is what you do for a living. It does not ask about your profession. Your **profession** is what you have been specially trained to do. The question does not ask about your **vocation.** Your vocation is what you feel called or specially and divinely appointed to do.

_____
_____
_____
_____

2. Are you living out your purpose? If not, why not?
(Did you just give an excuse or a legitimate reason?) Ask yourself if any reason is legitimate enough to let you go on living in misery or un-fulfillment.

_____
_____
_____

3. What is your timeline to begin to live out your purpose? (write down actual dates)

_____
_____
_____
_____

PART 3

Dos, Reviews & Deliverance

Chapter10

Taking a Second Look

Day 31

How much do you remember to practice?

The following revision of the steps to purpose makes it clear that one needs to focus on "purpose" rather than mere personalities or even character traits. If you walk that path of purpose earnestly, you will be driven, empowered and become engaged in marvelous ways that will definitely impact others as well as your community.

I have done many sessions on purpose, vision, goal-setting et cetera, with groups of various sizes. The groups also consisted of people of different ages and different socio-economic background. Invariably I would ask this open question – "How many of you know what your purpose in life is?" I would usually follow that question with this: - "What is that purpose?"

I have always found that whenever I asked those questions, there is hardly anyone who could honestly answer that they know what their purpose is. Interestingly though, many of the persons in these groups are gainfully employed. They have jobs that they enjoy, they have families that they care about, and they are "law-abiding" and charitable citizens. Yet they would openly and honestly say, "I do not know what my purpose in life is."

If you really want to find your purpose and be set free by it, then your journey will look like this: your focus is purpose then your journey begins as follows:

1. Reasons for your being

You ask yourself, "Why am I here?", "Where am I going?", "How can I get there?" These three questions help you to define your very essence. You seek to orientate yourself in reference to a universal compass prompted to make some important moves that will line you up with your God-designed blueprint.

2. Your skills

Once the first three questions are answered, you need to look at what you have and ask, "What are my skills? That is, what have I been trained to do?" Then you must look at your talents. You must therefore ask yourself "what natural abilities do I have?" Then you must ask yourself "what tangible things do I possess – what are my resources?

3. Observe Needs and Problems

The third step towards discovering your purpose is to look at the needs and problems around you. Pay attention to the issues in families, in the neighborhood and in the wider community. Once this takes place, the windows to the soul, the eyes (or the intuition) will open up, and you will see the probabilities and possibilities all around you.

4. Use your Unique Skills and Talents

The discovery you make at steps 3 should lead you to think of ways that you can use your "unique" skills, talents and resources. Only you can do what you are able to do exactly the way you do it. An important part of the process of discovery is dialoging and consulting with the community about ways in which you can serve. Once this step is taken care of, then the functional question arises – "When shall I begin?"

5. <u>Get Involved</u>

Starting is important. You need to get involve. Get involved in finding a solution to the problems and to the needs around you. This starting point will likely open the door of self-discovery. Here is where you become acutely aware of what drives or calls you. Such a drive can grow into something deeper.

6. <u>The Intense Drive</u>

The intensity of a drive – That is, the sense of call, may even take on compulsive qualities. You think about it all the time. You mentally rehearse your role. You get creative with what you have to do. You must then examine this sense of compulsion and carefully note the ways in which it may lead towards doing what is helpful and good.

Sometimes, that which is helpful and good may not be expedient. In fact you may find it to be costly and inconvenient. On the other hand, you may turn out to be an unintentional pioneer. If this last step (step six) is fully pursued, you will eventually shout Eureka! Eureka! – I have found it. You have found the thing that makes you tick; the thing that you are sold out to; the thing that you cannot help doing.

Even when that thing becomes burdensome and it drains your energy, it also becomes the very thing that re-energizes you as you do it. You may become physically drained at times by what you do. Yet your soul will find rest and you will enjoy an inner peace when you pursue that good thing, which you have become captive to.

7. **Happy Discovery**

You have finally discovered who you are. You give what you have. And you do what you must. At this point you become, as if by natural progression, willing to die for something. Also at this point you are more able to visualize how you can make the world better. You no longer struggle with thinking about your purpose. You know what your purpose is. You can now think through with great clarity, the unfolding process of living out that purpose.

Many people function well in our world today. They are gifted, they are skilled, and they help to make things happen in the world. This is good. Nevertheless, many people gravely underperform, because they have not discovered their purpose. They are merely living out a given model. To put it another way, they are merely living in reference to a model that has been given to them.

Like Jesus before the start of His public ministry, many people live below their true potential. Their "blue-print" is yet largely unconstructed and therefore unrealized. It remains a work of art by the master craftsman instead of a building worthy of the very thought that the master invested in the drawing.

Notes:

_____

_____

_____

_____

_____

_____

Chapter 11

You Must Know

Day 32

No guessing!

"Purpose" seems rather evasive both as a concept and as a living reality for a large number of persons. Yet a life that is set free by purpose beams lustrously as the rays of the sun, calling attention to itself and impacting the world. And like light that is known yet illusive to define, so is purpose.

Write your definition of purpose

_____

_____

_____

_____

_____

The person who is set free by purpose wants to make a positive, helpful and needed impact on the lives of those who become a part of his/her life. He also wants to be impacted by those persons so that he can be a better person. He sees the people in his life as necessary contributors to how he works out his blueprint in the world. On the other hand he sees himself as a vital part of the outworking of the other persons' blueprints.

So there is a kind of dance that takes place here. It is a dance in which each person's life influences the other person towards the fulfillment of his/her destiny. Unfortunately we miss many lessons and opportunities because we shut our minds (and sometimes ourselves) off from the persons who do not match our preferred images. This is usually the result of fear, ignorance, insecurity or plain laziness on the part of those who close the door to dialogue and interaction.

The affirmation we make in this book is this: *For the person who sees his/her life as a ship,* **purpose is his captain. Purpose is the igniting agent** *that enables a movement in a good direction.*

* Write the statement above in your own word. Imagine that you are explaining the concept to someone who has a little more difficulty than you are, in understanding what I just said. Note the images of a *Ship* and a *captain*.

_____
_____
_____
_____
_____
_____

When I moved to the United States of America, I wanted to discover places of interest while trying to find my bearing in what seems to be a confusing place to get around; because up seems to be down and down seems like across, et cetera. As I engaged people in discussions about ways of orientating myself, a few persons suggested that I "get myself lost" so that I could learn my way around. Now, why should I do that when maps are made to keep people from worrying about getting lost?

It seems much more prudent for me to look at a map, plan my route, and then board the bus or the train to a desired destination. Then I can relax and enjoy peace of mind having a sense of where I am, where I'm heading and how to get back where I started.

The life that is driven by a sense of purpose and intentionality is liken to the stranger in a city, who plans a tour of that city; and then she goes ahead with certainty, confidence, and raw vigor to utilize the transit system.

Purpose is connected to precision. The more one is driven by a sense of purpose; the more precise, thorough and time-efficient he or she is likely to be. That person learns to be calculated and at the same time flexible and spontaneous. He or she may even procrastinate when faced with a situation sometimes. Such deferring of action in the moment is done in order to make a better call; or to use better judgment later on.

Finally, we ask again, what is the nature of the seemingly evasive concept of purpose? The process of discovering your purpose is a struggle. Every great leader, whether religious or otherwise has gone through a period when they agonized over their mission or their sense of call.

It was in that agony that they experienced their defining moment. Then they moved on to make notable conquest. They saw (i.e. they understood) that they needed to change lanes, or change location or even change occupation in order to move closer towards their purpose.

If you find a "mission" in life with only an earthly frame of reference, you may do well in planning, preparing and producing, thereby impacting the world. If however, you understand that your ultimate aim (purpose) is to give glory or pleasure to God, then you will explore ways of doing well on earth for the reward of having God say, "well done my child."

I continue to be amazed at the extent to which Christianity fails to help its adherents to bridge the gap between works and grace. On the one hand, the Christian belief system is grounded in faith. Christianity says that human beings are utterly lost, disconnected from God, and unable to connect with God in the way humanity should. Hence we can attain the bliss and the security called salvation when we accept Jesus Christ into our hearts by faith and when we trust in the grace of God alone to make us utterly right with God.

On the other hand, the Christian holy book the Bible is clear that we are saved unto good works. Hence, even though we become saved or accept God's salvation apart from our good works; we still need to be actively working for a reward in both this life and the afterlife.

Notes:

_____

_____

_____

_____

_____

_____

_____

_____

Chapter12

Deliverance: How it Works?

Day 33

Are you a champion in chains?

I encourage you to review the scope and the essence of Purpose. I also give necessary attention to the principle of faith and Freedom. The hard truth is, if a professional fighter is placed in a ring with an amateur or totally inexperienced fighter, it is possible for the inexperienced or amateur fighter to badly beat the professional. How is this possible?

The reason is that some condition must exist that prevents the professional fighter to fully utilizing his skills and knowledge to defeat his opponent. This is what the concept of deliverance addresses. It acknowledges that sometimes good and capable people are kept from being their best because they are beset by unseen, yet real forces which are at work in the world.

One of the important principles highlighted in this book is that you must include the idea of God in any serious and profound discussion on purpose. For this reason I submit this additional note for critical reflection. Simply put, we are compelled to examine the attributes of God in the broadest concept of God and with reference to the vastness of God. This will lead us to discover who and what God really is.

Since this book is by design a practical self-help tool; and since you have done a fine job at working through the exercises in the book; let us raise the stakes as we comb through the bible. So here is what you should do

– Write each verse of the scriptures in your own words below the printed words from the bible. Also, where there is a second or a third person pronoun that relates to you, insert your name. For example, if the scripture say "The Lord shall favor you". You must say, "The Lord shall favor _____ (insert your name here)".

Let us get going then, with the scripture references:

God is a counselor to _____*(Dillon/Mary)* (psalm 16:7)

Example: God wants to talk with me when things are bothering me.

God is a deliverer (psalm 70:5)

_____

God is righteous (Deuteronomy 32:4)

_____

God is the creator (psalm 139:19)

_____

God is holy (psalm 22:3-4)

_____

God is just (Isaiah 45:21)

_____

God is a stronghold in the day of trouble (Nahum 1:7)

_____

God is a refiner (Malachi 3:2-3)

_____

God is a healer (Malachi 4:2)

_____

God is a purifier (Malachi 3:3)

_____

God is sovereign (2 Samuel 7:28)

God is peace (Ephesians 2:14)

God is the Author of faith (Hebrews 12:2)

God is Radiant (Hebrews 1:3)

God is pure (1 John 3:3)

God is all-knowing (John 16:30)

God is wisdom (1 Corinthians 1:24)

On account of who God is, we must conclude that the worship of God is the ultimate means by which we learn what our purpose is and how to live out that purpose to its fullest. So in a sense, when we acknowledge and worship God we give ourselves a gift. And that gift is the key to unlocking our purpose.

You must remember that Planning leads to preparation which leads to production. Production is geared towards fulfilling us existentially. Ultimately however, the essence of purpose is that we pursue God. In the process of doing so, we find our true self. We give pleasure to God when we fully use and express our talent and fulfill our potential for the highest good.

Purpose can only be truly discovered when a person enters into union with his/her creator. God as creator takes a person through a process of discovering who and what he/she really is. The discoveries of that journey line up and add up to paint the picture of what is in God's mind for people.

I admit that it is difficult for some people to come to terms with this connection between God and purpose. It is difficult for some people to entertain God in their conversation or thinking period. It is for this reason, that the most prolific writer and missionary in the Greek Bible says in Romans 1:20-21 "For since the creation of the world God's invisible qualities—his eternal power and divine nature—have been clearly seen, being understood from what has been made, so that people are without excuse. For although they knew God, they neither glorified him as God nor gave thanks to him, but their thinking became futile and their foolish hearts were darkened."

Many people do not discover or achieve their purpose in life because of negative energies and forces that inflict and affect them. These forces are called by different names such as Enchantments, Divinations, Spells, Hexes, Curses, Witch craft prayers, and idle words spoken contrary to God's original plan and design for a person's life.

In the Bible, the apostle Paul talks about the forces in terms of their hierarchical structure. Paul says in Ephesians 16:12 "For our struggle is not against flesh and blood, but against the rulers, against the authorities, against the powers of this dark world and against the spiritual forces of evil in the heavenly realms".

The point here is that we humans do not live alone on planet earth. In fact, certain people are so aware of this that they have learned how to tap into the spirit realm and put evil forces to work in other people lives. For this reason, some people try hard to live out their purpose, but their way seems to be blocked on every side. Sadly, many people are not aware of this because they have not been taught these things. And sadly, the church does not teach any real depth of spirituality.

Unfortunately, the church by and large teaches its adherents to be good individuals according to a set of rules and traditions. It teaches them to observe certain good practices that will help them to build up their spiritual disposition and to learn to love God more. Sadly however, it barely, if at all addresses the issue of spiritual wickedness and the ways in which adherents and believers can counter these evil works. It is like an athlete who strengthens one of his legs and totally ignoring the other. That athlete will run into trouble in a matter of time.

In deliverance, believers use words such as loose, bind, cancel and rebuke. They take authority over these forces of evil; and destroy them or send them back to the sender or to their source. Sometimes, deliverance has to take place in the context of a gathering in which believers and their leader who is skilled or gifted in the art of spiritual warfare will combine to overthrow the evil force.

Usually the leader or someone else is gifted by God with the ability to identify the evil force, otherwise called the demonic spirit. That person is also gifted to speak to the spirits as if they are speaking to a real physical person. The person then uses specific word, commands, prayers and gestures to wrestle the demon out of the affected person.

The action of deliverance always involves prayers and Holy Scriptures. It may often involve oils and water. There are even times when the situation calls for something unexpected and unusual. I once heard of a situation in which the pastor asked for a glass of water to be given to the afflicted person. After the person drank the water, she was instructed to smash the glass and throw it away.

Having shared these insights with you, let me offer you this prayer offered by Evangelist Heather Lashley. She ended with this prayer one night, at the end of one of the sessions she led for us on spiritual warfare at Harmony Tabernacle:

"Father I thank you for tonight and I thank you for your word. O the entrance of your word brings light. O God it just brings such encouragement. It makes me love you again and again and again and again. That's why I makes me brag; and rave, I show off because I have a brand-name God.

Art thou not God? Hallelujah! Glory be to Jesus. Hallelujah. Are you not God in heaven? And do you not rule over all the kingdoms of the nation? And in your hand is there not power and might, so that no one is able to withstand you? Are you not our God, who drove out the inhabitants of this land before your people Israel and gave it to the descendants of Abraham whom you called your friend forever? O God, You are this God for me, for my children, for my ministry.

We know that you are God – Deliverer God, Provider God, protecting God, healer God, great God, almighty God, and strong God. Even now God you are going back to our homes with us. We see you high and lifted up. We see you greater now than you were yesterday, and earlier today. You are the God of the mid-night hour, the God of the 1 O'clock hour, the 2 O' clock hour, the 3 O'clock hour. Whatever the devil is operating in; you are God of that hour; hallelujah! And we praise and we bless you.

We give you glory and we say to you almighty God: Thank you, thank you, thank you, for being our God - A god that is going to pay every bill; a God who is going to heal every sickness, affliction, disease and infirmity; a God who is not only going to fight every battle; but you are going to win them in the name of Jesus. You are champion of champions, hero of heroes, and giant of giants. O god you are healer; the almighty God; the immutable God, the infallible God; the infinite God and the faithful God. You cannot deny yourself and you will not deny yourself.

Thank you for my family, my ministry, my privileges and joys, my fellow laborers and ministers; bless us and keep, strengthen us, and preserve us. Empower us to fight the good fight of faith. And give us the faith and the courage to trust that you are the God of the spirits and *men, you are the God of every angel - you are God over demons and holy Angels. You are the victorious Father; and I put our households in your hand; those in this place and outside of this land. We trust you for healing, deliverance and protection **in Jesus name. Amen.**"*

You may include my own addition of thanksgiving as Follows:

*"Thank you Lord for breaking the chain and the spell of spiritual wickedness that has held me back for far too long. Thank you God for the fresh anointing that I have received. Thank you for the new path and the new direction that you have set me on. **Glory be you your name forever, Amen!***

I commend this prayer to in all sincerity, with the confidence that it will give you a sense of power as you say it over and over again. In addition to the prayer, I offer you the following decree that my wife, Carlene developed for our family. We have it in large print on the mirror of our Dressing Table, so that it is before us all the time. This way, we could read it often without going to look for it. You have my permission to copy and enlarge it, for your use in the same way. Here is that decree:

I DECREE AND I DECLARE

- *That Almighty God is the only head of my life.*
- *That I am the righteousness of GOD; covered by His blood; hedged in by His love and protected by a host of angels.*

- *That no weapons formed against me shall prosper and any tongue that rises against me in judgment shall be condemned.*
- *That my children are a Royal Priesthood, called, anointed and appointed to function as Prophet, Priest and King to the glory of GOD.*
- *That my children and their children; and their children's children; and each succeeding generation shall know and serve GOD all their lives.*
- *That my family and I have been favored with health, wealth and wellbeing.*
- *That the Ministries to which my family is assigned, and the ministry that we birth, will grow the lives of all who become a part of it; and it shall grow beyond any of our dreams to the glory of GOD.*
- *That all our financial debts are paid–in-full.*
- *That I am indebted to no one save Christ and Him crucified.*

I am convinced that God really wants to establish and equip his child to be mighty warriors in the spirit. We must be constantly on guard against what the Bible calls "familiar Spirits". In order to develop this fighting ability within you, God will allow or cause you to go through great difficulties. This will accomplish two things. First, it will make you better fighters in the spirit. Second, it will show you what you more clearly what your ultimate calling and purpose in life is.

In this period of difficulties and closed doors, you will come to the realization that the doors that were close to you had to be closed in order for you to look for and to look at the ones that you should really go through. Thankfully, in this intense looking, you see and you find those doors. And with enough determination and courage, you enter them. This is an important point.

Sometime ago, I went into New York City. I had an appointment at a certain office. I arrived within the vicinity of the building in which the office is located. I could see the building ahead of me. I was heading towards the building, but I still got lost. I stopped to ask direction from the nearby security guard. He redirected me around the building, since the path that seemed obvious to me had actually come to an awkward end where the road was being repaired. Eventually, I got to the building. I stood before the door and rang the bell. I was buzzed into the office. Then I had to be escorted to the inner area where the actual office to which I was going is located.

Sometimes the door you are looking for is located behind a series of other doors. But you will find that special and particular door, if you do not proceed to and through the ones that you see.

The difficulties that you face on this journey of becoming a good fighter and a person, who is set free by purpose, will force you to clarify your values and priorities. On my own journey, my difficulties made me to look deep within myself. I had to determine that I must strive to be in no one's debt - neither their pocket nor in their "you owe me" book. I determine that I must be favored. Thus any kindness or resources bestowed upon me must be favor and gratitude, not bribe nor inducement.

If you courageously decide to go on this journey, God will reveal to you the extent to which the Kingdom of Satan and the Kingdom of God are warring for your allegiance; and ultimately for your soul. You will soon discover that something is wrong with your spirituality. I discovered that I was not at my spiritual best. I was missing something. I was hungering for more of God and for a deeper and richer spiritual life. I did not quite know how to achieve this.

Previously, I had consulted various books on the spirituality, spiritual rituals, uses of the psalms, uses of oils and incense etcetera. But being careful to please God, I tried not to practice any ritual that I felt was not in line with true holiness. I am sure that sometimes I travelled pretty close to the border line. Now I can see the light of God clearer. I started learning all over again how to let the Holy Spirit guide me into all truth. I am more surrendered in the spirit; and less driven by ambition and the pride of life.

Sometimes, we can try too hard to help God. We need to learn how to surrender to God, so that we could be truly directed by God in God's way and in God's time. When we try too hard to help God, we pay a high price for doing so. Then we invariably beg God to fix what we destroyed or damaged.

It is better to have a life of solace and peace. It is better to have fewer but more focused engagements. It is better to endure hardship while seeking God's wisdom. It is better to learn how to adjust your ways, your views and your actions. All this is better than to resist, to react, to undermine, and to subvert any process or any movement that is threatening your ambition and endeavors.

There are times when you may need to resist, to subvert and to circumvent processes and systems in your sphere of influence. However, you cannot afford to be merely reactive. You must seek God more deeply through prayer and solitude. In doing this, you will need to pull away from people and from certain circumstances for a period.

Sometimes we try too hard to reach out to people who we think can help us with the situation we are facing. We need to stop being so busy trying to fix a problem instead of praising God in the midst of our problem. I discovered this principle in the midst of a rather intense moment of anxiety and fear when I could not figure out the solution to a gigantic problem. I tried intensely to focus on what God might be up to in my life. I began to praise God in spite of the situation. I had a serendipitous experience of learning at my heart level, that when I looked at the size of my God, I became less anxious over my problem. In contrast to our big God, our problems are quite small.

Chapter 13

Epilogue

Day 34

Are you free? Freedom has a Price.

I had a recent experience in which I was forced by circumstances to let go of a business venture in which I had invested a lot of time and resources. I travailed and agonized over the decision to let go of this project. However, I knew I could no longer hold on to it. I let it go. I then discovered how freeing it is for a people to let go of some of the load they hold so dear, even when they know that it is has become an unbearable millstone around the neck.

The irony of this whole situation is, on one hand I was enjoying the freedom from the load that was weighing me down. On the other hand however, I became confused, crippled and frustrated by the fear and anxiety. This was because I could not figure out how I was going to make it through with the bare essentials I was left with.

Financially, everything failed all around me. All I had left was God. I was taken in the spirit to the experience of the Hebrew people in the wilderness. Just as they were dependent on God for daily manna that fell from the heavens, I was depending on God daily for money. That is a very hard place to be. It is the place wherein you know that anything is possible, everything looks and feels impossible; and nothing is quite predictable.

In this dark experience and the terrifying darkness of a bright sunny day, I learnt that God is faithful. This had to become more than an intellectual and theological reality for me.

I was lonely, afraid, and sick and tired of being vulnerable. Yet I discovered that you cannot deeply learn certain valuable lessons about God and about yourself; until you find yourself at that dark place. In that place, you are forced to clarify your values, your priorities, your calling, your earth assignment, and your assignment in the heavens. Step by step, God gives you revelation. You learn to praise God and to thank God more than you ever did; rather than spending the most of your energy trying to fix things, and increasing your anxiety about what you cannot change in the moment.

The concept of being set free by purpose is to be understood in two ways. First, we humans are purposely set free by God. We are set free to be our best selves. We are set free to even disobey, disown, or even disbelieve in the existence of God. Nevertheless, God has set us free to occupy the earth and to be creative. God has done this because we are made of the substance of the earth. Therefore, God would not want to keep us in any sphere of the universe that will not favor our fullest development. I say this mindful of the fact that humans are amphibians.

Humans are both spirit and flesh. However, we have to make room to reason according to the Biblical account of creation and the fall of humans from a great relationship with God. In this regard, we can simply say that humans showed that they are more inclined o go the way of the earth – a sort of lower existence than heaven, as represented by the Garden of Eden.

The second manner in which we should understand the concept of being set free by purpose is this: We are only really free to be and to experience total fulfillment when we discover our purpose and live in it. In this regard, purpose set us free to be our fullest and best selves.

When taken together, the two points above show us the power of purpose. In my own experience, I have made some radical shifts in my life and ministry. Whenever I have made these shifts, I have always observed how colleagues, peers and supervisors mentors question my motive. Some blatantly express their disapproval of my decisions. Others ask in some "caring" and "brotherly" way, why have I chosen to go in this or that direction. In those times I have known that I was the subject of many conversations and some official or fraternal meetings. But always, I have been convinced that the host and company of heaven were having the highest level of conversation about me.

There is nothing like the freedom of thought and the freedom of mind by which you can pursue your blueprint. There is nothing more liberating than knowing that you do not have to lick boots, kiss bottoms or suck up to the masters in order to become who God has preordained you to be. I believe that I have come to a higher level of understanding what the apostle Paul was pointing to when he said *"For God knew his people in advance, and he chose them to become like his Son, so that his Son would be the firstborn among many brothers and sisters"* *(Romans 8:29, NLT).*

O what freedom we forfeit when we spend our time waiting for the year of retirement and the years of pension from a job that we neither like nor enjoy. What freedom we forfeit while we wait for a promotion to a particular office. And what freedom we forfeit while we bask in the mere safety of the familiar company and traditions into which we have been programmed. O that each of us would pursue **our** purpose, and then become overtaken and overwhelmed by it; and then finally become empowered by it; and live in it.

Appendix A
Further reading and study

For further study, look up the following passages of scripture in your Bible. Analyze their meaning for you. The comments alongside the verses highlighted below are my own. They are merely pointers for emphasis.

a) Acts 26: 16 God comes near to us for a special purpose – to show us our real mission in life. (*[16] 'Now get up and stand on your feet. I have appeared to you to appoint you as a servant and as a witness of what you have seen and will see of me)*

_____

b) Acts 27: 13. We must be careful how we interpret what appear to be signs to lead us to our purpose. (*[13] When a gentle south wind began to blow, they saw their opportunity; so they weighed anchor and sailed along the shore of Crete).*

_____

c) Proverbs 20: 18 The wise counsel of others must aid the journey towards one's purpose. *(Plans are established by seeking advice; so if you wage war, obtain guidance).*

_____

d) Acts 27: 43 There will always be someone who will show up at the right time to fight off those who seek to block us from fulfilling our God-directed purpose. (*[43] But the centurion wanted to spare Paul's life and kept them from carrying out their plan. He ordered those who could swim to jump overboard first and get to land).*

_____

e) II Timothy 3: 10 Awareness of your purpose will help you through your challenges. It will also inspire you to be an attractive example of virtue. (*¹⁰ You, however, know all about my teaching, my way of life, my purpose, faith, patience, love, endurance*)

---

f) II Corinthians 1: 17 The twists and turns that you make on your journey towards the fulfillment of your purpose will depend heavily on whether you proceed according to outer motivation (flesh) or inner motivation (spirit).

The apostle Paul has something encouraging to say to us. This great apostle was and still is the quintessential mirror of a Christian and an evangelist. He had fought many battles both figuratively and literally. Yet he came to a startling realization that there was a war going on within himself which was unlike any war he had ever seen.

That war was reflective of the war that every Christian has to fight daily. Paul calls it a war between the flesh and the spirit. He said "the good I want to do, that I do not do. And the evil I do not want to do. That I do. So if that is the case then it is the sin within me that is responsible for this war" (Rom 7:13 ff).

We too (even if you are not a Christian) live with the struggle of trying to choose goodness according to the higher principle and the moral law that is at work within us; and the need to gratify the fleshly desires which are driven by the pleasure principle.

An encouraging note from Paul assures us that the Grace (i.e. favor and blessings) of God will give us the strength to overcome and to succeed.

<u>Leaders Guide</u>

In this section, I offer you a biblical guide for further study on the subject matter of purpose. Primarily though, this is a leader's guide for seminar, retreat, and Bible study series. This section is a concise guide for a leader who wishes to use this book as a resource for a purpose seminar, a bible study series or a retreat. I myself have used it with a group and found it to be an eye opener and a good tool for encouraging participation by all group members.

I trust that this guide will prove an invaluable tool for many leaders to help people discover purpose and the overwhelming joy and fulfillment that come from that experience.

Introduction

The leader may begin by introducing himself/herself. Thank the participants for taking the time out and for making the effort to attend the seminar. After this, share a brief overview of the purpose of the seminar with the participants. Your overview may sound something like this: "Many people are gainfully employed. Many people keep busy with all kinds of activities and events. Yet many people are unhappy and unfulfilled. Most of the things they do are meaningful and help others. Yet something is missing from their lives and they know it. Today, we have come aside to address this question in a deep and personal way. This seminar is not a quick fix for anyone who is eager to find fulfillment in life. It is the section of ***Freedom airport*** where you collect your ***strategy boarding*** *pass*, proceed to the ***radical shift departure lounge***, exit through ***gate redemption (meaning - take back)***, and take ***flight purpose*** to your God ordained destiny. Destiny here refers to your fulfillment of your earth assignment. So forget any thoughts about utopia or heaven for now. Are you ready for the journey?"

Lead the group in a prayer. Alternatively, he/she may ask a volunteer to open in prayer. The prayer may be accompanied by a period of silence and centering as the participants in the group empty their minds of the distractions in their lives and get ready to deal with the matters of priority in the context of purpose. After this centering moment, the leader should proceed with the following questions.

It is important that the leader do not ask people to introduce themselves and to say a lot about their personal lives and professions. This is to avoid any prejudices and to keep the group process as pure as possible. The leader may do such introduction and sharing after the seminar.

1. - How many of you know your purpose? Share your thoughts and impressions about the graphics on the book's cover. What message does it convey?
2. How do you get a book to become a best seller? The answer is, they have an organization. Think of your favorite best-selling author. What organization, church, media group or television shows he/she has appeared on or is associated with?
The purpose of this question is to get the group to think about the power of being organized and of having an organization or a network.

3. Take a quick look at the stairway at the back of – P.U.R.P.O.S.E. Discuss the steps. The leader must allow ample time for this. It is recommended that you do not try to do this in one session.

4. Review: a) the eraser b) paper clip c) post-it pad Gently encourage participants to share their stories. If someone gets choked up, do not rush to tell them its O.K or to tell them not to cry. Let the moment happen.

5. Conclusion:

To conclude the session or the seminar, invite people for prayer. Within your group there will more than likely be at least one person whose story fits into the category of the eraser, the paper clip or the post-it pad. The following suggestion is one way to invite the participants by category.

You may also want to invite them to stand in the gap for people in their lives who fit into one or more of these categories:

• The eraser people – you can start over

• People who are stiff and unyielding – need to be flexible in the hand of God

• People who need to profit from their mistakes – the richest place in the world is the cemetery.

* get ready to start the support group (women against crime etc.)

* Rom 8:28 "All things work together for good to then that love the Lord …."

• Song "Spirit of the living God fall afresh on me"

Scripture references:

Make full use of the scripture references throughout the book. Also you may utilize the stories and scriptures ones below in addition to others that you may have prepared with your particular group in mind:

Murderer, Adulterer & lover of God
- David Killed yet he was the "man after my own heart" (The 1st and 2nd books of Samuel).

Messed up wise man
- Solomon was loved by God even though he messed up (1 chronicles. See chapter. 28 & other passages)

Helpful Harlot
- Rahab was a harlot yet she was saluted for her role in saving the lives of the spies from among God's servants. (Joshua 2:1ff)

Impetuous But loyal pioneer
- Peter denied Jesus. But his denial was matched by opportunities for restoration. (John 21:14 ff)

Repentant Adulterer
- A woman was caught in adultery. But Jesus gave her a chance to amend her ways by the power of God so that she can start over. (John 8:1ff)

Appendix C

Contact Info:

Ways for you to connect with us on an ongoing basis:

On the worldwide web at:

www.pastorburgin.com;
www.thepowerandfreedonofpurpose.com

Email pastor Burgin at pastorburgin@yahoo.com

You may also contact us by phone at 1- 347-378-2461.

Our other products include PB caps and T-shirts and gift baskets to express your love to the special people in your life.

We also have a variety of CDs on spiritual warfare. Other cds contain sermons on a wide variety of topics. Ask about it when you call or write to us.

Seminars and Conferences

You can access various seminars and conferences facilitated by Pastor Burgin conjunction with the Rising Stars Outreach center family and the Harmony Tabernacle family. The way to get in on these events is by visiting the websites noted above. You can also call the information line given above.

Additionally, you can make use of the social media network by connecting with pastor Burgin on *facebook*.com/pastorburgin;and on and on *twitter*.com/propastorburgin.

Seminars include:

The abused woman workshop

This is a forum for women who have been abused as children. Many women have been abused and molested by close relatives and by trusted friends. They still carry the scars of those encounters. Hence, many of them suffer in silence because they do not have a safe and non-judgmental place in which to let go of their hungry ghost and find healing. These series of workshops make this possible.

The stone leadership project for youths

This is a ten week project that teaches young people leadership skills and socializing skills; and prepares them to be high achievers in society.

The power of purpose conference

These dynamic conferences help the participants to gel with a community of people who like themselves, desire to grow beyond their disorders, their tendencies to procrastinate, and their confusions and setbacks that prevent them from being their best selves as God designed them to be.

Conferences are held throughout the year. Interested persons must visit the websites noted above for upcoming events and dates.

Peer Reviews:

Pastor Burgin has demonstrated by his work in this book, that some people are indeed called and anointed like John the Baptist from the womb, to do the work of the kingdom of God. These are the people who are truly free from the bondages of systems and tradition. This book truly challenges the reader to seek a freedom beyond mere religious systems and self aggrandizement.

Evangelist Heather Lashley, founder of *****

"This book ranking among most books is the best in providing the essential tools to for individuals to become successful in their lives. It has the distinction to be used as a guide to overcome daily challenges".

Wellington C. Ramos, Adjunct professor at Boricua College

"Pastor Burgin has demonstrated an extraordinary sense of purpose and direction in his book. This is a must read for everyone searching for spiritual and practical enlightenment".

Vincent W. Beale Jr., Business owner and Investor

Seven steps or levels to purpose

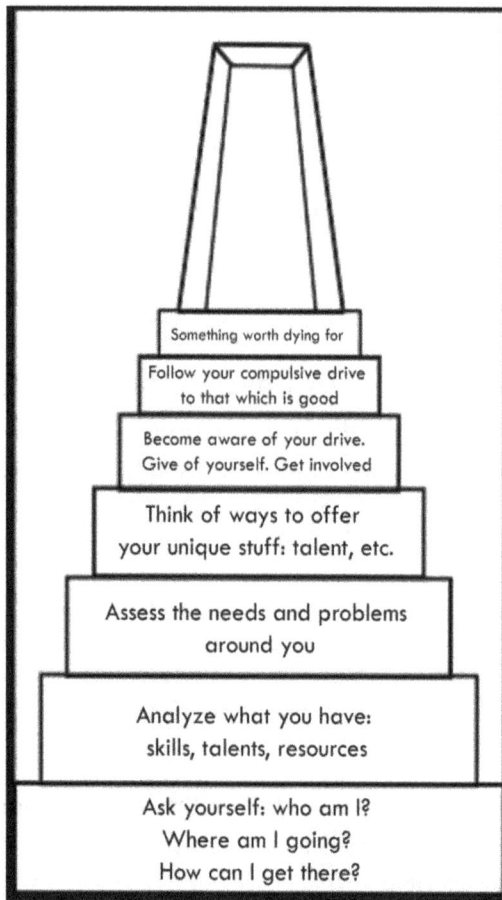

Something worth dying for

Follow your compulsive drive
to that which is good

Become aware of your drive.
Give of yourself. Get involved

Think of ways to offer
your unique stuff: talent, etc.

Assess the needs and problems
around you

Analyze what you have:
skills, talents, resources

Ask yourself: who am I?
Where am I going?
How can I get there?